GOD's Words
to Inspire the Angel in You

**Volume 1 of GOD's Words
details the first 12 of GOD's 20 Requests**
in 39 divine essays revealing how to achieve your spiritual ascension.

Note: Volume 2, entitled *Heaven on Earth*, details requests #13-20 in 40 of GOD's divine essays revealing how to save the enviroment and create Heaven on Earth.

Copyright © 2001 by I AM

All Rights Reserved, including translation in the USA, Canada and other countries of the International Copyright Union and under Pan-American Copyright Conventions and Universal Copyright Convention. No part of this publication may be reproduced in any manner whatsoever without written permission except for the inclusion of brief quotations consisting of up to seven entire, uncut, unedited paragraphs that are embodied in articles or reviews which must include this book ordering info: "Reprinted with permission from *God's Words to Inspire the Angel in You*; Volume 1 of God's Words, by I AM, copyright © 2001. Available from: www.IAMLOVE.TV for $19.95 - Free Shipping Order toll-free: 1-800-795-3069."

Please contact the publisher for permission to translate, reproduce, or purchase books at quantity discounts.

Publisher's Cataloging-in-Publication
(Provided by Quality Books, Inc.)

AM, I
   God's words : to inspire the angel in you / I AM. -- 1st ed.
   p. cm. -- (God's words ; Volume 1)
   LCCN: 00-190450
   ISBN: 1-892177-44-7 (8.5x11 hc color)
   ISBN: 1-892177-14-5 (8.25x11 pb b&w)
   ISBN: 1-892177-49-8 (7.5x9.25 hc color)
   ISBN: 1-892177-71-4 (7.5x9.25 hc b&w)
   ISBN: 1-892177-35-8 (7.5x9.25 pb b&w)
   ISBN: 1-892177-24-2 (6x9 hc b&w)
   ISBN: 1-892177-45-5 (6x9 pb b&w)

   1. Merit (Christianity) 2. Conduct of life--Religious aspects--Christianity. 3. Ascension of the soul. 4. Angels. I. Title.
BT773.A45 2001   234
                       QBI00-330

Book layout and Cover design by I AM

Published by
Heaven on Earth
P O Box 398
Hanalei, Hawaii USA
**Tel: 1-800-795-3069
e-mail:
GODSWORDS@IAMLOVE.TV**

Inquiries of GOD welcome!

God's Words to Inspire the Angel in You are also available on:

Audio   ISBN 1-892177-25-0
Video   ISBN 1-892177-27-7
CD ROM ISBN 1-892177-26-9
e-book   ISBN 1-892177-61-7

download direct from
IAMLOVE.TV

I AM

A note from the author...

I would like to tell you just a little bit about my life, so you can know who is bringing forth God's Words in His Own Name. For most of my life, I thought of myself as separate from God. And although I loved Him very much and honored Him, I did not understand where He was. Even though Jesus said, "The kingdom of God is within you," still, I did not realize it. I thought that God lived high off in His heavenly clouds looking down over me. It did not occur to me that He was here within me all the time.

When I was sixteen years of age, I experienced death. I must have been poisoned, because I became so violently ill that I did not have the strength to stand or walk. My sister carried me up the stairs and laid me in my bed. I wretched and dry heaved until I became so weak I couldn't move at all. The pain and sickness were unbearable. And then, everything went black. I saw a spotlight focused on the back of a man's head. Slowly he turned around and I was horrified to see that it was the Devil, and he was laughing at me.

I prayed for Lord Jesus to help me. Suddenly, it seemed as if I were at the bottom of the ocean with a whirlpool sucking me down. I couldn't breathe. I swam, struggling against the current with all my might. It took every ounce of strength I possessed. As I rose, I noticed that the water got stiller towards the top and easier to ascend. Above me, I could see the surface. I swam on until at last, I broke through where I could breathe.

To my astonishment, I kept ascending right up through the peaking waves. I looked down, and in complete surprise, saw what I had believed to be the ocean was the atmosphere of Earth. I had risen above it into space. I could see the whole world below me. It was infinitely beautiful to behold. I looked towards the sun and it was magnificent, so brilliant! Then I saw, in the far distance, two beautiful Angels shining brighter than the sun. They were flying towards me. A thrill of joy went through me as I thought, "They are going to take me to God." How beautiful they looked. They were the most beautiful beings I had ever seen, and yet, I didn't even have eyes to see. I didn't have a body at all, just a point of consciousness that could behold all the wonder and beauty around me.

When I started out towards them, I heard a Great Voice within me saying, "Wait there. You do not understand how it is." The Voice was kind, compassionate, infinitely loving, neither male nor female, pure, all-powerful, yet gentle... a Voice that seemed to come from the heart of eternity.

As the Angels came closer they spoke, and their words rang all around me and through me. "It is your Father's will," they said, "that you return to Earth. There is something of utmost importance that must be done during your lifetime, something that only you can do." I thought to myself, "Who, me? What could I possibly do that could make a difference?" And then it dawned on me, "Oh, they must have a case of mistaken identity. They have confused me with someone else, someone important."

The Angels said, "Do you want to do your Fathers will?" I felt disappointed, because I really wanted to be with God more than anything. Yet, there was no way to argue with a question like that. "Yes," I thought. "I do want to do my Father's will." And, as I resigned myself to His will, I suddenly sped through the atmosphere until I came to a stop, hovering just above my house.

I had super vision and super hearing! I saw my friend asleep in his bed through the rooftop of his house, three houses away. I could hear his dog breathing. In awe, I began to look around. Then I heard the Angels again; "Do you want to do your Father's will?

As I thought, "Yes," I descended through my rooftop, hovering near the ceiling above my dead body. Surprisingly, I was repulsed by it. Although I had enjoyed my life, I had no desire to go back into that cold lump of flesh. Then, I heard the Angels asking me again, "Do you want to do your Father's will?" And as I thought, "Yes," I suddenly flew into my body. I was stuck, and it felt as if I weighed a thousand pounds, considering a few moments earlier I had the freedom of weightlessness. I was tired, so very tired, but I thanked Jesus because the sickness was gone and I was safe.

What I had been brought back to Earth for, my mission, was to bring God's Words to you now, so you may feel the direct personal experience of His Divine Love. It is God's Will that people everywhere receive the benefit of His Divine Guidance, so everyone can experience the peace, the blessed abundance, and absolute joy of Heaven on Earth now.

I focused on God a lot through my life, and when I was younger, He spoke to me occasionally, always with miraculous consequences. My life was spared on numerous occasions, from horrific car crashes to attempted murder. By listening to God's Guidance, I have overcome many seeming tragedies and recovered from crippling connective tissue disease. When doctors gave me no hope of recovery from an autoimmune disease that landed me in a wheelchair, I was led by God's Unerring Guidance to a remarkable recovery. I have endured many broken bones, including a broken back, and all these have healed completely. When I was healing, I had more time to focus on improving my spiritual life, so I made God my full-time job.

In 1991 I focused on Him five to seven hours each day for nine months. Each morning I hiked up a remote sea cliff an hour before dawn. There I sat in God-Contemplation* for an hour before sunrise. Every day I felt His Divine Love and experienced ultimate peace. I reached the breathless state and experienced cosmic consciousness. Occasionally a few friends would join me in my early morning meditations. After one particular meditation one of them asked if he could interrupt me while I was meditating. I told him not to, for there was nothing in the outer world more important to me than this time "alone" and "at-one" with God.

The next morning, God opened my eyes the exact moment the sun began to rise, so I could behold His Light. Dolphins gathered by the hundreds in the sea below me.

* Words are defined beginning on page 229

Motionless, they floated, their dorsal fins rising above the surface of the water. This was the first time I noticed them. Instinctively, I rose and stretched forth my hands to bless them. Then they all jumped at once, spinning with glee. Beyond them, families of great Humpback whales gathered, and closer in to the shore, ancient sea turtles clustered together below me. "That's what I wanted to show you, only yesterday they just laid there! my friend beamed! Above me, giant albatross' circled overhead, while my horse and little dog stood at attention before me. They all lined up for my blessing, for they loved receiving the gift of God's Pure Energy. I spoke aloud, blessing the creatures of the air, the land, and the sea. Then my blessing also reached out to you, flowing all around the world, gracing each and every person, and blessing all life everywhere.

Earlier, in 1981, Jesus had come to me in Spirit. He said, "I want to come through you." Thinking that He wanted to be born into the world again, I got pregnant that very month. I gave birth to a son, whom I called Jesse Kuhio Kalani (which means, God's gracious gift, a prince of Heaven). Jesse is, indeed, heaven sent. He is so filled with nurturing love and helpful wisdom that at Hana grade school, his class made up a special award, to honor him for being the most caring and sharing child in his school. But, ten years later, in 1991, when I was blessing all the world, Jesus came to me again, exactly as He had in the past. Again He said, "I want to come through you." Confused, I said, "I gave birth to Jesse so you could walk the earth again." Then Jesus said with extra emphasis on the last word this time, "I want to come through <u>YOU</u>."

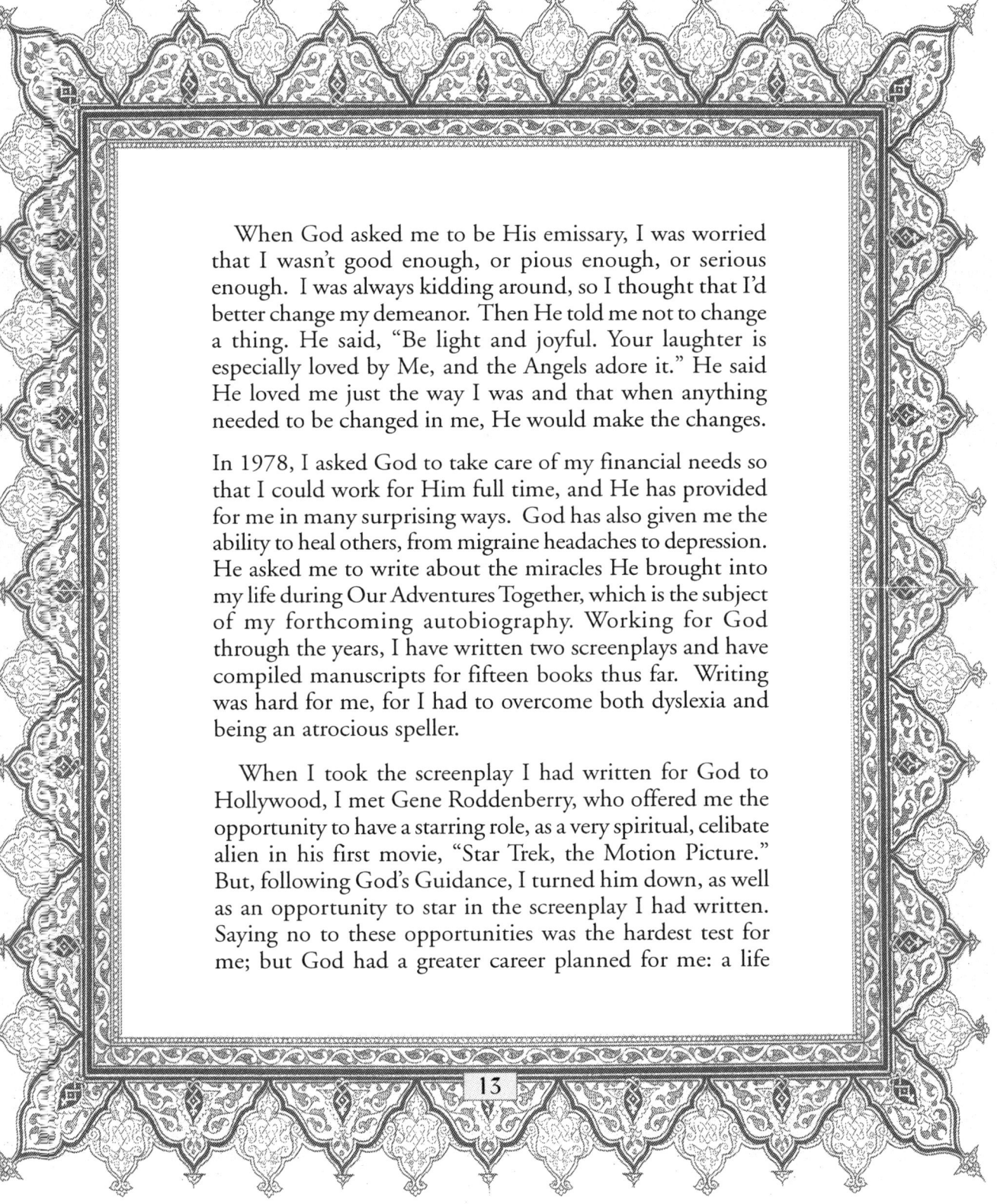

When God asked me to be His emissary, I was worried that I wasn't good enough, or pious enough, or serious enough. I was always kidding around, so I thought that I'd better change my demeanor. Then He told me not to change a thing. He said, "Be light and joyful. Your laughter is especially loved by Me, and the Angels adore it." He said He loved me just the way I was and that when anything needed to be changed in me, He would make the changes.

In 1978, I asked God to take care of my financial needs so that I could work for Him full time, and He has provided for me in many surprising ways. God has also given me the ability to heal others, from migraine headaches to depression. He asked me to write about the miracles He brought into my life during Our Adventures Together, which is the subject of my forthcoming autobiography. Working for God through the years, I have written two screenplays and have compiled manuscripts for fifteen books thus far. Writing was hard for me, for I had to overcome both dyslexia and being an atrocious speller.

When I took the screenplay I had written for God to Hollywood, I met Gene Roddenberry, who offered me the opportunity to have a starring role, as a very spiritual, celibate alien in his first movie, "Star Trek, the Motion Picture." But, following God's Guidance, I turned him down, as well as an opportunity to star in the screenplay I had written. Saying no to these opportunities was the hardest test for me; but God had a greater career planned for me: a life devoted only to Him, far away from the distractions of the fast-paced, worldly, city life, where I could become divine by focusing my attention on God alone. He showed me a vision of a beautiful paradise, a pristine beach where the sun rose from the sea with a hillside pasture for my horse, SunDancer. So I moved to Kauai and after some searching, found the promised land.

In 1996, God asked me to record His Words for the new millennium verbatim. He asked me to bring a little hand held recorder when I came to commune with Him, rather than later trying to remember what I thought I had heard Him say. God also asked me to change my name to I AM. It was challenging, because I felt people would scrutinize me, or think I was crazy, or judge me as being egotistical for claiming I was God. Oh, how I wished He had asked me to build an ark instead... (not that I could have!) But now, I am happy that I did change my name and I know He's happy too, because every time I meet someone in His Name, I AM, the conversation always leads straight to God.

I AM is God, because the Great I AM is alive and conscious in everything, as everything. Every one of us is divinely blessed to be part of God's unfolding miracle of love and life. I feel so reverent to know that I am part of God, that His very Spirit is at the core of my being, that He talks to me, and guides me, and gives me His Divine Love. Now He wants to do that for you too.

People often ask me how I hear God. When I was younger, talking to God was like a one-way telephone conversation. I did all the talking and then hung up with a reverent "Amen." One day, I was inspired to listen. I decided to still my thoughts. It is impossible to think our own thoughts and hear God's Thoughts at the same time, because He will never intrude upon our thoughts. And so, I had to really focus on listening and not let any thoughts come to mind. It was hard at first. Sometimes He would only give me one word and I would have to wait for ten minutes to get the next one. And then, when I got a word wrong, one I thought He was going to say, or a thought came to mind getting in the way, He would stop. Then I would have to go back and see where I had gotten it wrong and begin again. He was very careful not to let me get any words wrong.

At our core, every one of us refers to ourselves as I am, though usually in the context of "I am hungry," or "I am full." God created us in His Image and His Divine Spirit lives in us, as us. When we seek His Inner Guidance and choose to do His Will, we become godly. By contemplating God's Divine Nature and feeling Divine Love, we eventually become divine personalities who identify with God's Holy Spirit, rather than thinking what we have been taught to believe, which is that we are ego based identities, unworthy of and separate from God.

When we experience a divine merger with God's Indwelling Spirit, we are elevated to the joyous throne of Heaven within. There, we celebrate a Divine Marriage of Sacred Spirit, and become Temples of the Most High Living God!

I have aligned my will with His Will, and my soul is filled with His Holy Spirit. I realize that I AM God's Living Temple. I have invited Him to speak up whenever He likes. Now, He wants to speak through me, to everyone on Earth.

At the burning bush, when God asked Moses to free His enslaved people, Moses asked God, "Who shall I say has sent me?" God replied, "I AM." Moses didn't understand, so God repeated, "I AM that I AM." But God could not get through the rigid constructs of Moses' ingrained beliefs. Moses could only conceive of God as Jehovah: angry, jealous, and wrathful. He was, to Moses, the God of the fiery volcano, who vented while Moses delivered the Ten Commandments to the Hebrews. That is the reason there are so many conflicting views of God's nature within Biblical scriptures. Jesus knew Moses' interpretation of God's nature was incorrect, so He taught that the One True God, whose name is I AM, is our loving Heavenly Father who resides in the Heaven within our hearts. Jesus said, "The Kingdom of God is within you."

Jesus realized God's presence within Himself and received God's Divine Love and Guidance directly. He spoke God's thoughts, proclaiming, "I AM the light of the world." He tried to explain to people, saying, "These things I tell you, I say not of myself. It is the Father within me that doeth the works." But, unless people have had a firsthand experience of God within themselves, it is a very hard concept to understand, especially when they have been taught to believe that God is a mighty fearful Deity that lives somewhere else. Believing it was heresy and blasphemy to profess union with God, many people thought Jesus was egotistically speaking about himself, and so, misunderstood His teachings and condemned Him. Jesus said that we are all sons and daughters of God. Yet after His death, people who didn't really understand what Jesus was trying to say wrote the Bible. Consequently, they referred to "God's chosen people" as being the Hebrews exclusively. In fact, all people are God's people and for those who are enslaved, God always does His best to inspire someone to set them free.

God wants each and every one of us to have an intimate love-relationship with Him. It is possible for you also to merge with Him and develop your power to heal yourself and others. Jesus said, "These things and greater things shall ye do also." Let us prove Him right by creating Heaven on Earth now in this new millennium, for "God's Kingdom will come, when His Will is done, on Earth as it is in Heaven."

God's Providence
(God speaks from this time forward)

Dear One,

This is the Divine Providence* of the New Millennium. This is going to be the most splendid time, for all of those who have sought to know Me and love Me. I AM here for you now, My Blessed Ones, and this Divine Manuscript shall be the beginning of My Talks, which shall bring you the guidance you need to achieve divinity. In these days you are surely ready to begin the Ultimate Quest for Perfection, which will bring you to My Door and into My Loving Embrace.

Let Heaven be manifest upon this blessed Earth within the next decade. May all of My Children, in every land, hear My Words and understand what it means to have their Father-Mother God here to Bless them now. Do not feel that you cannot attempt the ascent into Godliness, for surely I AM with you now. And I will help you, My Chosen Ones, to become the Divine Children of Heaven you were always meant to be.

And so, take this wise council from your Lord this day. And please do your very best to understand the ramifications of your Divinity upon this Earth. For surely, you, as My Divine Heirs, shall create the Blessed Gardens of God, which will glorify this Earth and bring her into a state of Paradise never before known. For all the world can now be blessed by you, My Children everywhere, as you gather yourselves together to reforest this land and regenerate My Divine Garden once again.

And so, make it your priority to accept the responsibilities that Godliness brings, and help Me. Fulfill My Requests of you by making a firm pact to begin anew together, all My Dear Ones, to create Heaven here. For surely it is only an erring misconception to believe that Heaven is somewhere else. Didn't Jesus bring you the good news that the Kingdom of Heaven is at hand, and that the Kingdom of God is within you, and that My Kingdom will come when My will is done on Earth as it is in Heaven? I know that these concepts clash with what you have been misled to believe for so many years. But I tell you in truth that the old concept of Earth being separate from the rest of Heaven, My Dear, is only a misconception, just as people once believed that the Earth was flat. Now you know that your Earth is one of many, many heavenly bodies that comprise My Glorious Kingdom.

Earth is a Paradise Estate, destined to be a Jewel in the Crown of Creation. And so, My Dear Ones, rise up and take your place as My Blessed Heirs, and together, reclaim your paradise home. For in so doing, you shall create abundance beyond measure. And all of this glorious wealth shall be embraced, as you use it to provide the basic necessities of life to everyone, as you also provide the Glorious Love of True Brotherhood. My Blessed Ones, it is time to take your place as the Divine Sons and Daughters of Heaven. Do begin this day to follow My Guidance and the Words I have brought forth for your benefit so that you may attain your birthright and become the godly citizens of Paradise.

GOD's Words
to Inspire the Angel in You

Volume 1 of God's Words
details the first 12 of God's 20 Requests
in 39 divine essays revealing how to achieve your spiritual ascension.

Table of Contents

I AM ascendiing..6
A note from the author 7
God's Providence 19
Legacy of the Heart 27
The Holy Attribute of Divinity 31
Fortitude 35
God's 20 Requests 38

Become Divine

The Divine Plan for Humanity 63
Spiritual Beauty 71
My Divine Presence 75
My Gardener 77

Live by The Golden Rule

The Golden Rule 81

Be Harmless

Be My Divine Emissary 87
My Beloved Creatures 91

Purify Yourself

Addiction to Drama 99
Alcohol 107
Drugs 109

Be My Living Temple

Become the Temple of the Living God 113
God-Contemplation 115

Use My Name Righteously
I AM Your Divine Identity 123

Love Me
The Treasure of the Ages 131
The Divine Director 135
Love Me 139
Why People Suffer 147

Love One Another
Holy Company 155
Challenging Relationships 159

Bless Your Enemies
Be Merciful 165
The Past 169
Peace 171

Love Your Family
Love Your Parents 177
Romance 181
Sexual Intimacy 187
The Path of Right Choosing 191

Worship Me above material things
Graven Images 197
The House of the Lord 201
Find your Security in Me 205

Bring Me Your Devotion
The Quest 211
The Holy Sacrament 215
The Holy Covenant 219
Divine Worship 223
Walk with Me 225
Definitions 229

Legacy of the Heart

Dear One, Hear Me now:

I AM most pleased with this accomplishment: My Holy Book for all the ages. Yes, it is, in truth, the Divine Manual for the Ascension of Humanity from lowly mortal will-creatures of time and space to the Supreme Spirit Residents of Eternity.

This Divine Revelation of the True Nature of God is the most fortunate Revelation ever given. It is, indeed, the Legacy of the Heart, which has found a way to be enthroned in the lives and conduct of My Blessed Ones of Earth and Heaven. My Testament of Divine Love will flow out as a Grace to nourish all My Beloved Children everywhere.

My Heavenly Angels do bid you well on your complete understanding of the Divine Attributes of Spirit which are set forth herein. The 20 Requests are made at a time when this world is in a state of peril from environmental destruction because of wanton acts of sin, greed, and degradation.

I would have you know that each and every word of this Beloved Masterpiece comes from the Heart of God through the Divine Interpreter, who is the Heavenly Mother aspect of the Paradise-Trinity. She has embarked on this adventure of Divine Intervention as My Emissary to bring forth these Sacred Doctrines as a Blessing for all Humanity. To you who are reading these words, know that it is through Divine Intervention that they are brought to you.

My Holy Presence, operating through the mind of My Dear Emissary, has enabled this Divine Perspective to come into being. My Words are pure, My meanings evident.

Therefore, know this to be true: These are My Perfect Words to Humanity. So read them with the knowledge that I AM here with you and that My Spirit also dwells in your mind and, as you are reading, will assist in your complete understanding of My Holy Words.

This Revelation is My Profound Gift to you, My Blessed One, and it is My Divine Objective to keep this Book whole and uncorrupted throughout time.

The Holy Attribute of Divinity

Dear One,

Let us begin this day to unravel the mystery of the Soul and reveal what steps need to be taken to bring the Soul into alignment with Spirit, which will bless the Soul with the ability to become Divine.

Divinity is the ultimate realization the Human Soul must strive for to become God-realized. Divinity is the Holy Attribute which will bring God-likeness into every endeavor. The emanation of Divinity expressed by the Soul clothes the Spirit in a Radiant Garment of Light. This Divine Raiment is the most beautiful garment that could ever be worn, for it is the personification of the Holy Attribute of Divinity.

Divinity is the fulfillment of the promise of potential within each emerging Spirit and is the basis for God-Realization, which will be forthcoming by your earnest efforts to express these Sacred Attributes. There is a little known, yet highly acclaimed, discipline which will lead to the perfection of one's Soul. This discipline is to realize the Godly Attributes of Divinity and express them Joyously.

GOD-/GODDESS-hood is an endowment of Spirit which is gained through the Right Use of All Resources. When you express Divinity, you become ennobled, and your raiment, which is your Garment of Light, glows in brightness, perceptible to all other Spirit Beings. Your Divinity is plainly shown for all to see, and it is this clothing of the Spirit in Divine Light by which you will come to be known in the ages of the future. So realize that each time you choose to express Divinity, your Spirit is clothed in a more beautiful radiant garment.

Some on Earth can actually perceive the Halo of one who is expressing Divinity. Seeing the Aura is a Spiritual Perception. So try, in all you say and do, to uphold the Noble and Virtuous emanations of Divinity, which are the uplifting

Attributes of Kindness and Compassion. Divinity is expressed in knowing these virtues as a true measure of one's Self. Divinity is attained through the vigilant endeavor to choose righteous actions, thoughts, words, and deeds in every instance. The choosing of Divinity on a constant basis raises the moral integrity of the Soul to the status of a Divine Spirit.

Act in accordance with My All-wise Guidance and your Soul will prosper. As you choose to express the Heavenly Ideals set forth in this Divine Manuscript and bring these precious and ennobling truths into your life, you will gain many beautiful qualities. I will be here to assist at every turn, so please be kind and generous. Reach the goal of feeling compassion for every creature, large and small, and you shall radiate with a light more brilliant than the sun in the days soon to follow.

The Divine Self of an individual is an Everlasting Attribute of Spirit. I would have you know that the most important step you can make is to align yourself with the Truth and act in every instance according to your own feelings. Doing so will lead to the expression of the Dynamic Ideals of Truth, Virtue, and Goodness: the primary motivating factors in the Spirit-led life.

To be in the Light and come from the Truth in all areas of one's Life is the Principle Salvation of those who embark upon this noble and enlightening adventure of the Soul. It is the way each individual obtains Spirit Status and thereby gains Immortality.

The Divine Self leads to the gates of Heaven and beyond.

Become aware of this Ennobling Truth: My People of Earth must learn of this Godly Attribute and become Divine by their own volition.

Fortitude & Perseverance

Divine Ones,

Fortitude is the attitude of the Soul to persevere until the Divine Objective is reached. Comprised of determination and courage, it will enable you to proceed through all adversity to accomplish the goals I ask you to accomplish now. Fortitude is a true measure of stalwart determination. It is a requirement of character gained through earnest efforts in the pursuit of excellence, which hallmarks the emerging Divinity of the personality centered on Godhood. I would have you immerse yoursef in this Divine Attribute.

I will Bless you abundantly as you proceed along the course that will bring you the Glory of Heaven on Earth. There is much to be done, many forthright endeavors to pursue, and through Blessed Perseverance all shall come to pass and the Glory of God will reign in Paradise and Grace your lives with Abundance and Joy.

So take heart and dig in that you may achieve this great and glorious goal. Heaven shall be established on Earth as God's Will is done by your purposeful crusade. Create this Blessed Kingdom for the Glory of your Lord and begin the Golden Age of God.

The Gardens of the Lord shall be pristine in beauty. Your handiwork will adorn this earth with loveliness and bring great joy to all. Your Father in Heaven does thank you for your sincere efforts and perseverance in bringing forth this bounteous treasure of Spirit in the face of all adversity.

Spirit is as Spirit does, and the attitude of Spirit is staunchly rooted in the attitude of Fortitude. It is a Divine Attribute which must be developed by the emerging Spirit-Realized Personality of each and every Soul.

Fortitude is a Courageous state of mind, a Noble Objective to be achieved by My Beloved Children as you aspire to become Godlike in every way.

Expressing this Divine Attribute will infuse your whole being with self-confidence and surety that all can be accomplished through your valiant effort.

Divine Ones, blessings of many kinds shall be yours in the days to follow. I will be here to lend a hand to guide you all along the way. Please give all you have to this great endeavor and you shall live in Paradise on Earth. My Heart goes out to each and every one of you in this cause, the noblest pursuit humanity has ever undertaken in service of the Lord. The Angels applaud your perseverance and guide you in all your blessed endeavors.

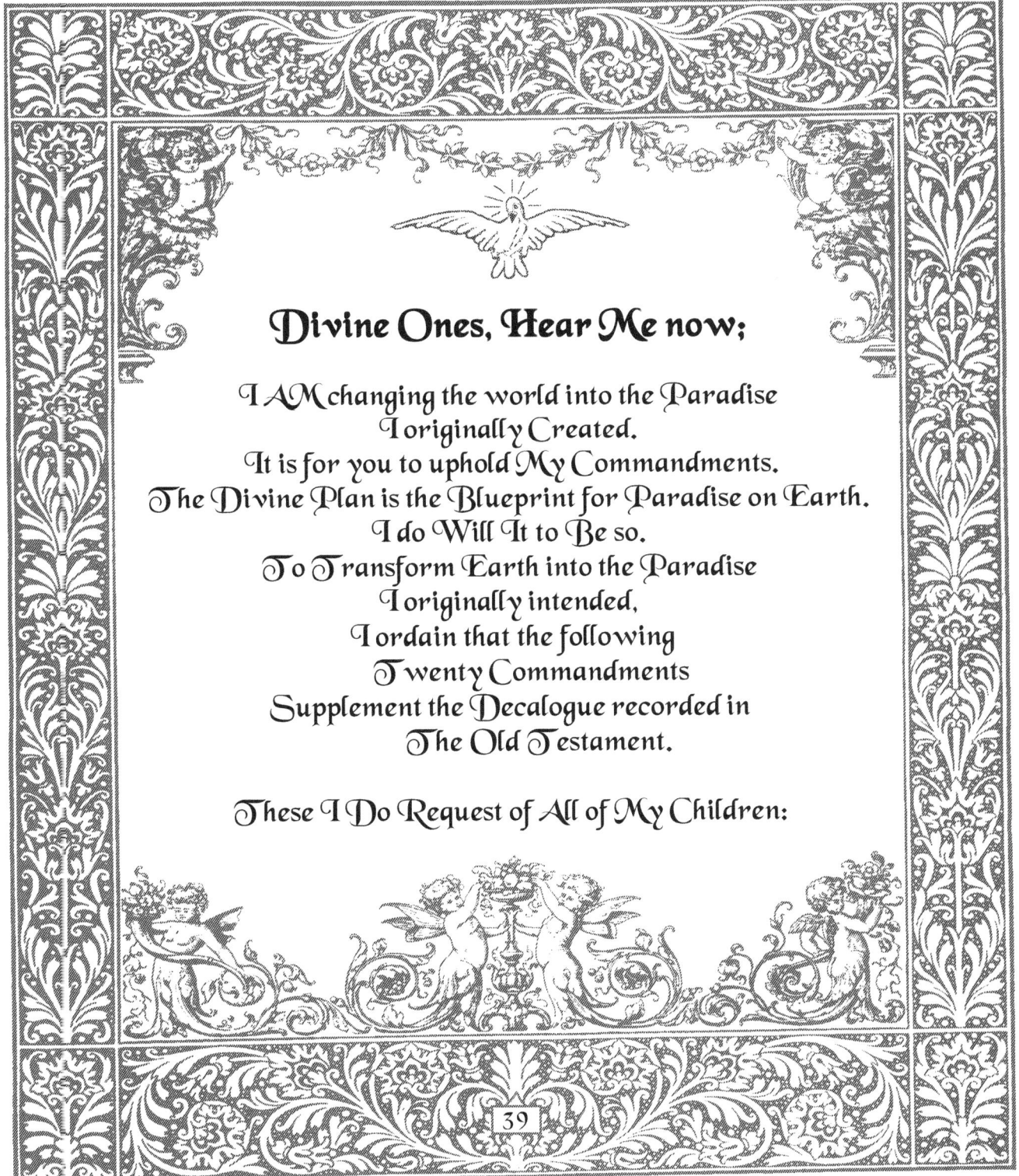

Divine Ones, Hear Me now;

I AM changing the world into the Paradise
I originally Created.
It is for you to uphold My Commandments.
The Divine Plan is the Blueprint for Paradise on Earth.
I do Will It to Be so.
To Transform Earth into the Paradise
I originally intended,
I ordain that the following
Twenty Commandments
Supplement the Decalogue recorded in
The Old Testament.

These I Do Request of All of My Children:

1
Become Divine

Become Divine, My Children,
embrace the willingness to become
all you were intended to be.
The Divine Image of God
is in each and every one of you.
So be prudent and fulfill your
Birthright to be Glorious.

2
Live by the Golden Rule

Treat others as you would like
to be treated yourself.
Moreover, offer unto your fellows
the Kindness and Mercy
I would give them under all circumstances,
and treat each one as you would treat Me,
for I surely dwell with
My Blessed Ones.

3

Be Harmless

Do not harm others.
Injury is painful, and
I feel everything My Creatures feel
as they experience it.
Give kindness to every creature that shares
this lovely Paradise home of yours.
I will foster every worthwhile action
and Bless you with
My Grace.

4

Purify Yourself

Take no dangerous drugs
or other poisons.
I will free you
from the bondage
of drug dependence.
Ask for My Blessings,
and I will help you overcome
these stresses to your immune system.

5

Be My Living Temple

Do this for Me:
Become the Temple of the Living God.
Let Me live in homes of love and kindness.
Permeate the atmosphere around you
with sweetness and gentleness, so I may find
a residence within your peaceful heart.
Live together harmoniously.
Loving Charity will mend all rifts.
Make your home the Temple of My Love,
for I do live there with you.

6
Use My Name Righteously

The least understood of all My Commandments concerns
taking the Name of the Lord God, which is I AM, in vain.
At your core, your identity is I AM.
And I AM in each of you, whether you realize it or not.
I have given you the power to create with your thoughts and words,
as well as the freewill to merge with Me and be Godly,
or to produce evil as the fruits of your life.
Watch your words, My Children,
for whenever you speak words of condemnation,
make negative assertions or think destructive thoughts,
such as "I am sick," or "I am broke," or "I am not perfect"
you create chaos and disease and fill your lives with misery.
Even though the situations you call into being
with your words do not immediately transpire,
that does not mean that they are not on their way.
So use My Name to create what you really do want
by making positive affirmations, such as
"I AM healthy, happy, and blessed forevermore with Love,
and the Grace to manifest my most cherished dreams and goals."
Thus you may use My Name rightly, not in vain.

7
Love Me

Find Me in your most precious heart
and bring Me the treasure of your Love.
Love Me with every part of your being
in every way possible, and I shall reward you
with a Treasure of Happiness and the
Freedom to stand up and lift your head high,
without guilt or shame.
The only original sin is the separation
from God caused by your own guilt.
Let Me free you from this iniquity.

8

Love One Another

Ask for and Give Forgiveness liberally.
Restore harmony.
Enthrone Love in your hearts for each other.
I AM the God of Love,
and I require Heaven on Earth now.
Make it so by exercising your
Godlike attributes to Forgive
and accept others unconditionally.

9
Bless Your Enemies

Do this for Me:
Don the garment of understanding
that shall end all conflicts.
Take the time to put yourself
in the shoes of your enemies.
When you have walked a mile
you will see that all feel the same.
I Love you so very much
and cherish your attempts to
Forgive and Bless your enemies.
Doing so is truly Godlike.

10
Love Your Family

Love your parents and treat them with respect.
Also, Love your children and treat them with respect.
For you are all My Children, My Blessed Ones,
and I do want you to be kind and considerate to each other.
Parents must guide their children to the best of their ability,
and children must fill their parents with hope for the future.
We all have Our parts to play.
Let it be in loving harmony.
Cherish each other, My Dear Ones.
Make your Love blossom and grow.
Embrace the virtues of Universal Brotherhood,
for you are all cherished members of
My Divine Family.

11
Worship Me Above Material Things

Make no graven images to worship.
This includes worshipping money
or the prestigious symbols of wealth.
I AM the Creator of Paradise,
and I do wish to be worshipped
by My Loving Children,
to whom I provide all things required
to live in happiness.
Love Me, not the items that bolster the ego
and thwart the spirit.

12

Bring Me Your Devotion

Bring Me offerings of flowers and fruits
rather than sacrificial or monetary offerings.
What I truly want more than anything
is your time spent with Me
in God-Contemplation.
Your devotion is My Fondest Treasure.
Bring Me this offering daily, and
I will raise you up to sit with Me
on Heavenly Thrones on High.

13

Make this world a Paradise

Restore My Kingdom on Earth by
repairing the damage to nature.
Clean up the toxic and nuclear wastes.
Restore My Rivers.
Make My World a
Pristine Garden of Delight.

14

Create Heaven on Earth

Do My Will, My Children:
Grow up to become
the gods and goddesses of Paradise.
Create Heaven on Earth.
Enjoy your lives, your families, and your friends.
Make your world into a world of splendor
and share My Love
with everyone you encounter.

15
Do Not Judge Others

Do not judge others' actions, for, because
of the forces acting upon them in their lives,
it is impossible to know why they do what they do.
So cast no judgment that puts others below you.
Send loving thoughts and Bless them so they may
rise out of the situation in which they are immersed.
Then they may be free to change their actions.
Send not guilt or shame,
for these squelch the impulses to do good and be happy.
Do not hasten to levy a judgment upon your fellows,
for even I do not judge the actions of My Children.
I would rather lift them by the hand of their own Divinity.
And how is Divinity accomplished?
By focusing on the Good and Forgiving the rest.
You must relinquish guilt and judgments to become Divine.

16
Sanctify Life

Do Not Kill,
Neither human beings, nor birds,
nor members of the animal kingdom.
They are all precious to Me.
I would rather have you
treat them with respect
and honor their lives
as you honor the life
I have given you.

17
Replant the Trees

Do
not take the
lives of the trees.
They are needed to
restore the balance of nature.
I would have every person now
alive plant an assortment of fruit and
nut trees. They will provide your banquet
in Paradise.
Propagate them and you will be blessed.

18
Live Naturally

Live naturally.
Grow a garden. Tend it well.
Recycle your waste.
Protect your home from pollutants.
Do not fear the coming changes
to your lifestyles,
but embrace them as the way
to continue to live on this planet,
for all must be changed
to reinstate the natural balance of nature.

19

Trust Me

Trust Me to provide all for your enjoyment.
Ask Me for what you desire.
Put your faith in the Creator of All Things,
both material and spiritual.
I shall be glad to work with you
to accomplish all
for a better world.

20

Ask and You Shall Receive

Do not take the property of others
without permission.
Ask and you shall receive.
Try it.
Ask Me, My Darlings,
and I shall be happy
to fulfill your needs and worthy desires.

Volume 1 Chapters

Become Divine	61
Live by the Golden Rule	79
Be Harmless	85
Purify Yourself	97
Be My Living Temple	111
Use My Name Righteously	121
Love Me	129
Love One Another	153
Bless Your Enemies	163
Love Your Family	175
Worship Me above material things	195
Bring Me Your Devotion	209

The Divine Plan for Humanity

Good Child,

Today I would like to bring your attention to the business at hand: Creating Heaven on Earth. Do follow as I elaborate upon this Divine Plan of Mine, for the accomplishment of this Supreme Goal will contribute greatly to the establishment of Heaven within the hearts of All My Beloved Ones.

There is a Destiny I AM bestowing upon your Blessed Soul, the unfolding of which will bring you Great Joy and open you to receive My Divine Gifts of Spirit, which you may incorporate into your daily life. They are Charity, Kindness, Grace, and Simplicity. Cherish these Divine Ideals as you enthrone them in your emerging Spiritized Personality.

The Divine Plan calls for a recipe of these Ideals to be mixed thoroughly and completely warmed with the Divine Light of Love: the Sacred Flame I do ignite within your Soul. This recipe for Heaven within one's own heart can be brought to simmer and be tasted, for the sweetness of the Essence of the Ascending Spirit you are becoming will savor of Heavenly Delight.

The true mark of attaining this Infinite Goal is the measure of Joy apparent in your splendid countenance.* Joy that radiates peace and kindness is a reliable measure of the realization of Heaven within one's heart. Do this for Me, My Beloved One: Bring forth the Divine Ingredients and mix them well, for it is truly said that "the Kingdom of Heaven is Within." Prosper yourself by cultivating this Spiritual Garden that bears the sweetest fruit, for the nectar of the Soul is the perfection of your Love. In time you will honor and cherish these Divine Ingredients as Sacred Endowments, for indeed they are truly of Heaven.

I AM bringing forth these Divine Attributes of Spirit so you may experience a perfect blend of Love, Faith, and Charity, sprinkled with a dash of Joy that will make the Dynamic Self you are divining* a delight to your every sense. For when you are immersed in joyful love and peace, kindness and compassion will radiate from you in a natural flow. Then you indeed house My Divine Spirit within your Immaculate Soul.

In this way you are truly Born Again, and you are not what you were. The old self, with childish whims and ego-based dramas, which embrace the dross of envy, pride, lust, anger, anguish, suffering, fear, revenge and regret – all these are relinquished and subdued as the Divine Self emerges from the Sacred Heart of a Spiritualized Individual. As you live the Divine Ideals which are motivating your actions, thoughts, words, and deeds, the ego recedes, thus the Kingdom of Heaven is established in your heart, and once the Glory of Heaven reigns in your Sanctuary of Divine Love, your lower self shall be conquered and your Higher Self freed to soar on Wings of Spirit, which lift you ever higher… to My Divine Embrace.

The Heavenly Ones do embrace you and bring you solace in times of need. These graceful Angels who populate My Heavens are bringing forth the Divine Attributes to Bless all Humanity at this time. The lofty idealism of these Celestial Personalities will bless you and cause you to grow in Spirit as they hold you ever up in their Majestic Minds and inspire you to do good and be happy.

My Beloved Ones of the Celestial Heavens, the Angels hovering ever so near you, rejoice at your comprehension of these Words of Mine. For you do enter the Kingdom of Heaven by embracing these Divine Ideals and wholly establishing them in your daily life. The Angels applaud your lofty idealism, which is the hallmark of the Divine Being you are becoming.

It is true that the Kingdom of Heaven and the Sanctuary of Divine Love may only be attained through the constant emanations of Peaceful Joy and Divine Love. They are the required vibrational frequencies of Spirit that must exist in the life of an individual on a consistent basis before he or she may gain admittance into the Heavenly Realms of My Grace. Only those emanating peaceful joy, which comes through the conversion of My Divine Love, can express this Divine Attribute of Spirit which is consistent with the vibrations in My Heavenly Realm. No disruptive vibration may enter My Glorious Kingdom, no disillusionment, no ego-dramas, which plunge an individual's energy field down, plummeting him or her into sorrow, anger, or lesser emotions. The vibration of Heaven simply won't allow it.

And so, to be in the flow of this Peaceful Paradise now emerging on Earth, you must find within yourself a place of consistent, serene joy. This joy comes by feeling My Divine Love, which initiates your Mystical merger with My Indwelling Spirit.

So do be cognizant* of the many times you create upheavals in your feeling-nature. Do this for me, My Beloved One, and you will see that your happiness is a constant feature of your emerging identity. This quality will be most pleasing to all, especially to you. Therefore, lift your gaze to the Realms of Godhood that are found within, and raise yourself up by the hand of your own Divinity. This I know you can do, for you are created in My Image.

There will be a time in the near future when you will discern* exactly where a person's heart lies. You will be able to discover the Hidden Treasure that you may extract from the mire of the illusionary world. This world is created by the ego that keeps one's attention focused on the lower nature and the difficulties it generates whenever it may. The Divine Treasure I speak of is the Perfected Personality, which finds its identity in the Spiritual Nature.

A Sacred and Majestic Fragment* of My Holy Being dwells within each and every normal mortal mind and serves to bring balance into the realm of creativity. All individuals will find themselves immersed in the sublime currents of Blessedness when they choose to express the Divine Ideals of Perfection in every way.

This is the Royal Road that leads to Godhood. There is no other path to follow that will take you to the Divine Embrace of Love. You may become a fully Spirit-Realized Being by choosing to express your personality through My Holy Spirit within.

So do try, at every turn, to enlighten all individuals to the cause of their misery. Express the Divine Ideals. Joy, Peaceful emanations, and Blessings are incorporated in the blossoming individuals who are becoming Spirit-Realized. By your own venture, you may find your Real Identity of Spirit, which lies dormant within your mind. For there is a Great and Abiding Presence living and dwelling there – the

Almighty I AM.

Try to see from the Cosmic Viewpoint, My Darling One. It is unnatural for you to be concerned with trying times, which cause the ego-bondage so prevalent in today's modern societies. I would have you begin to determine your Perfect Future with Me.

It will not be long before you display the Divine Attitude, which is Blessed Holiness. There is a time to embrace the Divine Directives and a time to be quiet and foster the Grand Scheme so that it may unfold for you. Contemplate your future. Decide how you would like it to be. Be diligent in your efforts and you will bring forth the Perfect Peace of Your Lord, which shall shine in your life, unquestionably gracing you with Heavenly Love.

Spiritual Beauty

My Darling,

It is wise for you to be the best you can be. Develop your natural gifts rather than trying to be the ideal proposed in a shifting, ever-changing sea of trends (in fashions, scents, and looks) that must be adopted for acceptance by society's standards of beauty.

There is no ideal model of Spiritual Beauty that is sought after in the world today. I would have you excel in all of the Blessed Arts of Perfection that you may embody. For your Soul has a beauty rare and fragrant, like unto the rose. When tended and cared for, you will flower into the most beautiful being imaginable. For you are truly that which is inside of you.

This passing life will go by so quickly. These fleeting moments when styles and trends seem important will pass away as surely as the sun sets. In time, you will come to know and appreciate the Purity and Beauty of Spirit which you are becoming. These are Treasures which will not tarnish with age.

Do try to spend your time focusing within and nurturing those qualities that bring you Divinity, for they are the Radiant Garment that you will wear when your Soul makes the great transition into a Body of Light. The raiment you will wear will clothe you in Perfect Adoration. No finer garment has ever been made. No fairer scent has ever been refined.

Care not what others may seem to notice, for those with small-minded, shortsighted perceptions only admire the outer garments which fade and tear and turn to dust.

My Darling, I would have you adorned in the Loveliness of Spirit. The Joy which never fades shall crown your Blessed Embodiment as you transcend this world and pass on to the next... on and on through My many Mansions, until you reach My Doorstep in the Central Isle of Paradise.

The Light of the Soul shines brighter than any star. I would have you wear the Glory of Godhood and crown you with the Jewels of Heaven. So be of good cheer and realize that when you endeavor to value the Beauty of Truth and respond to My Spiritual Guidance, you will embark upon a journey that shall bring you the Glorious Liberty of Divine Raiment. You will raise your scepter on high and call forth the Angels and Blessed Spirits who shall light your way.

So beautiful is the Spirit, so infinitely beautiful! Try seeing beyond the mortal frame. Look within and behold the loveliness and perfection of a heart and mind centered on Godhood. A heart and mind clearly expressing the Divine Qualities of Truth, Beauty, and Goodness, blesses all the world and shines on, far into eternity. Be My Beautiful Beloved One, whose Beauty does outshine the Stars of Heaven. Be this for me, My Darling; you are so lovely.

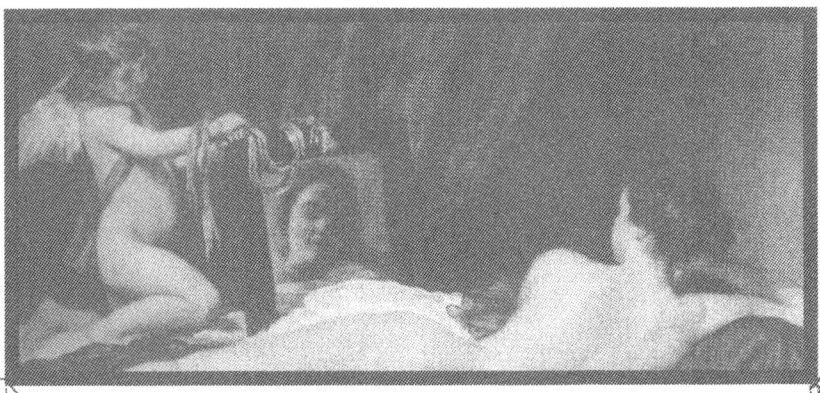

My Divine Presence

Fortunate One,

It is well that you do all you can to be kind, generous, and happy with everyone you meet. Always look for the beauty in others, for I AM within each one of My Children. When you see Me there, you may bring out the best in each one you look upon, for with your recognition of the Divine Spirit in each one, it is impossible for him or her not to recognize the Divine you see and rise to become that which is acknowledged and appreciated.

By seeing God in them, you may bring to their consciousness a whole new concept of Godliness, which they may incorporate into their persona.

When creatures become Divine, they will eventually free their ego-enmeshed personalities. Ego-emancipation clears the way for the reality of the Ascending, Perfecting Being that eventually takes over. Your Perfection is accomplished through association with the Divine, which I AM.

Seeing Me within others is the best thing you can do for them. I cherish this ability you have to see Me in the Souls of others. So look deeply in their eyes and behold My Divine Presence.

My Gardener

Dear One,

Blessed is the countenance of My Beloved One. It is a fine refrain* that fills the Heavens this day, for you are in all ways becoming more and more like your Father in Heaven. The Holy Spirit of All does grace you benevolently* with the soft caress of Infinite Joy and the tenderest Love which you display so willingly to each one you encounter. How wise of you to follow your heart in all matters and treat each one as the perfect Soul blossoming there, filling your garden with fragrant bouquets of the most cherished varieties.

Oh, the Souls of mankind and what they do know of the glories of Love! What hardships they endure as they grow on this imperfect world. It is often in the bed of such a garden that grows the most fragrant flowers, for they shine forth in the face of all adversity to become the most glorious blooms in all the Gardens of the Lord.

Tempt not the Gardener to display any of these fair and rare, fragrant roses and gardenias that bloom in the service of the Lord, for they are the most choice, perfect examples of the Blessed Spirit whose light draws their essence heavenward to grace the eyes of God.

From now on, whenever you see flowers turning their faces up to behold the Light, pause and fathom the Treasure of your Garden, the many delightful flowers whose Souls are blooming and opening to the Light of Spirit, the Divine Light they are reaching up to behold as I Bless Them with the Treasure of Eternal Life and Divine Glory.

The Golden Rule

Dear Ones,

Please follow the Golden Rule that Jesus gave you: "Do unto others, as you would have them do unto you." For the Golden Rule is My finest model for ethical conduct, which has endured through the ages and been advocated by every great spiritual leader throughout history. It is truly the cornerstone of morality. I would now bring a new and higher philosophy to add to the Golden Rule: "others" also refers to My Children of the Animal Kingdom.

I would have you realize that you have a shared destiny with all living beings on this planet. And the way you treat the Living Treasures of My Vast Kingdom is how you will be treated yourself. Whatever destiny befalls the sacred ecosystem will become the destiny of every living person as well. Should a species go extinct because of the folly of mankind, there will be one less Treasure in My Blessed Kingdom. For you all do share this beautiful sphere. I would have you all lead happy lives, filled with joy and exuberance.

Christ said, "Even to the lowest of these: when you do for any one, you do for Me." I would say the same in behalf of My defenseless creatures who are murdered for their pelts or meat or simply because you disdain their looks. Even the tiniest of these I do love. Gather yourselves together and realize that you are all kindred, for the Life I have bestowed upon you is the same Life that shines in the hearts of all of My Divine Creatures everywhere.

Hear Me now: I AM the Blessed Father of each and every one of My Countless Myriad* of Beings who live on every level of reality, as well as those who exist in the Spirit Realms on every dimension in My Kingdom of Light, where only the most Perfect Divine Beings do illumine the Glorious

Palace of the Heart. For I AM the expression of life everywhere present within all the many kingdoms of nature. Be they animal, human, or blessed Celestial Spirits, you all share My Life, which I have given you to enjoy. So do not rob others of this precious treasure and consider how you would feel if your life were shortened by even a day. Consider the lives of all of My Creatures sacred and you shall raise up your character to the Divine Spirit that you were born to become. Do this for Me, My Precious Heart, and one day you will realize We are One.

Blessed are they whose faces shine with My Joy, for they have applied the Golden Rule. I would have you discover the perfect ways you may bring delight to those who surround you and bring the Peace of your Lord to all you encounter as you go about your days.

It is fine for you to begin, in all that you say and do, to regard the tender feelings of others as a precious trust. If you are enabled to turn on the joy, which comes through understanding, then please focus your gifts of compassion upon all those who seek to be touched by your Divine Presence. Let Joy be the measure of your success, and let the Happiness you impart to others you are near be the gauge of your proficiency in the Divine Art of Being.

Be Harmless

Do not harm others.
Injury is painful and
I feel everything My Creatures feel
as they experience it.
Give kindness to every creature that shares
this lovely Paradise home of yours.
I will foster every worthwhile action
and Bless you with My Grace.

Be My Divine Emissary

Dear One,

When you are in a dangerous situation, and you or your loved ones are threatened by attack, I would have you look first at the intention of any violent person, marauding* mugger, or vicious killer who would have you be a victim. Could his intention be deflected in any way other than by killing the intruder? Is it possible to stun, but not kill? Would it not be better to avert acts of wanton destruction with the pervasive Power of Peace? I would have you always choose Peace. In many cases you can discover ways of dealing with hostile personalities that do not demand the ending of their lives, or yours.

When at all possible, please take defensive actions, which shall end conflicts without serious harm to anyone. These can be mastered through many techniques of self-defense and self-preservation. Many schools teach ways to end conflict suddenly without causing serious harm to the attacker. So do be wise and kind to all My Creatures, and you will find that Peace will become your life-style and threats will cease. Those who live promoting violence shall also die in violence. Those who promote Peace will attain My Heavenly Grace and sit by My Side in Paradise.

Dear One, it is wise for you always to begin each conversation with "Peace," and greet everyone you meet with this fine salutation. I will be there to encourage you each time you make this affirmation for Me. Beloved Peace is indeed what the world needs now. My Children, greet everyone with affirmations of Peace. Be liberal with your spreading of this fine, beneficial, and perfecting essence.

Peace does reign in the hearts of those who do My Will. It is well that you begin to treat every living being as you would like to be treated yourself. Doing so entails a great deal of thought and empathy, which is created by your ability to put yourself in the shoes of all those around you, whose lives you touch with your own. That includes all living things, from the tiny creatures of the insect kingdom to the glorious Angels who surround you and inspire you to offer love and kindness to all you greet. I will be here as a witness to every kindness proffered* to any of My Blessed Ones, be they large or small, winged or furred.

I will bless you abundantly for offering kindness to every creature and peace to your comrades and brethren. The peace in this world will grow as it spreads from heart to heart, bringing joy and the surety of peace to every country, until this whole world is brimming with Divine Joy and Peace pervades every heart.

There is a well, deep and abiding, which needs to be filled with the joy that you can bring to this world of Mine. So do become a Wellspring of Divine Joy and offer the nourishment of the Soul to everyone you meet. As a blossom gently opens and fills the air with fragrance sweet, so will your heart open to bloom and exude this divine essence of peaceful joy, which will enrich the very air you breathe and carry forth this blessing. Every creature, great and small, and every plant shall be deeply blessed by your peaceful emanations and joyful countenance.

Realize that All vibrates with My Divine Life, and everything that is, is part of Me. So respect all and treat everything lovingly. Extend love, peace, and joy, for these are the fondest Attributes you can share on behalf of the Divine Spirit which dwells in your precious heart.

I AM every thing that lives, breathes, moves and every thing that stands or creeps upon the earth. I AM perfect, and My divine creation seeks to express the Perfection of Divine Joy, which can be felt and known by all aspects of the emergent life within all the Kingdoms of Nature.

All things feel, and in Heaven We promote the feeling of peaceful joy. Bring Heaven to Earth, My Divine One, by your conscious actions to create this blessed peaceful feeling amongst all humanity.

Bless My World as My Divine Emissary in the truest sense.
Yes, bless each thing and do not harm anything,
for this is My Will.

My Beloved Creatures

Dear One,

Verily,* I would have you know that there are a vast number of beloved creatures in My Domain, here and scattered throughout all the universes, who are very dear to Me. I have a joyous plan of life unfolding for small creatures as well as the larger and more intelligent species such as humankind.

Many cannot fathom the idea of life being sacred for all My creatures. It is.

Even the tiniest insects have their part to play in the creation of a balance in nature. They are minstrels which serenade the night as the birds sing during the day. Hear them sing, My Love, serenading their Creator. I do Love them just as I Love all of My precious beings.

It is unwise to kill anything that I, your Heavenly Father, in My Divine Wisdom, have created to live on Earth. If you don't want insects around, there are less than lethal methods to discourage their attendance.

Remove the source of attraction and the ants will disperse. Cleanliness is next to Godliness. If you find roaches, spiders, or geckos, put them outside. Creatures prefer being outdoors. Escort them out and I will be pleased.

My Dear Ones, do try in all your endeavors to realize that I do Love all of My Beloved Children, so put not others below you, even those so meek. Help them to have happy lives and do not continue to poison them, for in reality, you cannot create a poison that will not turn on you. Every destructive and willful action, with which you cause the suffering and the demise of any integral species, will corrupt the whole system of natural balance, which I originally created.

So please, harm none of My Creatures, large or small, for they all have their parts to play in My Divine Kingdom.

Treat all of My Creatures as you would treat Me, for I AM also in the tiny ones who inhabit My Creation. Offer kindness, even to the smallest of these, and you will be richly blessed with a gift of sweet charity which will uplift your Soul to Divinity.

Killing is a hindrance to the evolving Spirituality necessary for the establishment of My Grace within the Soul. Kindly grant all of My creatures the life I have bestowed upon them.

All creatures finned, winged, or furred will be blessed by an Enlightened One. So do regard all with kind charity, and the Angels will draw near you, bestowing their blessing on the meek, the kind, and the beautiful Spirits of My Sons and Daughters who would not harm another of My Precious Creatures.

Do heed My Call and bring forth this Dynamic Principle into the world, for All Life Is Sacred. Every life I do bestow upon the Earth and in the Heavens has a purpose. And who is to judge whose purpose is greater or lesser than another's?

Be Kind

    We all have our parts to play in this Divine Kingdom of Mine. I would have you, therefore, adhere to the strictest principles of Harmlessness. Consider your Guardian Angels and take their lead; for the Angels harm not, and Bless all with their Divine Goodness and Intentions.

    You do not understand how animals that do not speak can have feelings, but, I tell you, they do. Their feelings are deep and rich, and I would have you respect them and treat them all as My Divine Children.

    Let everyone know that I have created this world for all My Creatures. And those who willfully take another one's life unnecessarily, that is for any reason other than to protect one's life, shall be judged accordingly when the Ancients of Days issue their unerring decree.

Addiction to Drama

Dear One,

Verily, it is wise to stop filling your mind with television shows that leave you feeling worse rather than better. For true happiness, fill your cup with My Divine Love and drink it into your perfect heart! You can use your leisure time to uplift your spirits, but do not rely solely on television for this experience. If you do not choose the shows carefully, they will simply fill your mind with thoughts of violence, fear, and morbid images you do not need in your consciousness at all.

How can you contemplate Bliss when I AM pushed into the background by thoughts programmed into your mind by television dramas full of intense pictures of hate, violence, and destruction? These violent programs are not simply a waste of time; they are designed to bring you down. Please realize that the only way to rise above despair and confusion is to have Wings that Soar on the Lofty Winds of Love, Peace, and Perfection. Do contemplate these by filling your mind with pictures of loveliness and beauty.

Addiction to television and movie violence is an addiction to drama. When you let go of that addiction, you can have peace and happiness. When you are programmed with negative dramatic situations, you tend to create them in your daily life. Doing so is counterproductive to right thinking. If happiness is a gauge of personal success, how happy can you be if you are always involved with this conflict or that drama sucking your attention and dragging you down? Not happy at all! This child's play is sense-addiction on the mental/emotional plane, which causes anxiety, stimulating the endocrine glands to secret hormones directly into the bloodstream, stressing your body as well.

See how often you get a stiff neck while watching riveting action and suspenseful drama. It is harming your cells. Those cells that are reproducing at the time you are undergoing stress become susceptible to mutations and are weakly formed. Stress exacerbates any on-going health problems.

Have you heard of the man who cured his disease by laughter? Yes, laughter is good medicine. You may delight in watching comedies and uplifting stories. Programs representing the beauty of the natural world are also beneficial, but be wary of the horrific stories that produce stress and muscle tension. For the body makes its own chemicals when the mind perceives stress. Viewing violent episodes on television releases adrenaline and other toxic substances which injure, age, and eventually kill the physical body.

Mental addiction to stress-producing drama has reached epic proportions. The horrific refuse being programmed into the minds of adults and children alike is an assault on the senses, the body, the mind, and the emotions. It is a clever way to control people's attitudes and feelings so that they will be fearful and depressed. This method of mind control is used by sinister people to keep good people imprisoned by fearful thoughts and feelings which are programmed in by scenes of death and destruction. This harmful programming is why inner city killings are so rampant. These young people are doing what they have been programmed to accept as real. Then they create their worlds to reflect this horrible programming. Twisted, greedy producers glamorize violence. Unscrupulous motives defile young minds with rampant scenes of death and destruction, violence and abuse, injury and decadence. These corrupt even the most stable societies and undermine the values and morality of goodness.

You can create peace and happiness in your life, but you must give up this addiction to drama, for it is an insidious drug that pollutes the air waves and ruins lives. So do this for Me, My Darling Heart, please plan what programming you will allow into your living rooms and which programs to let your babies watch, for they are so easily influenced and their brains do not distinguish between what is real and what is make-believe. Their subconscious lets in all the morbid waste, programmed in by devious minds, bent on the destruction of the spirit and the annihilation of the young. It would be wise to regulate the creation and exploitation of dangerous programming, which uses violence as a means to corrupt the youth and destroy the moral fiber of the population as it poisons the minds of adults and children alike.

By boycotting explicit scenes that teach children to be violent and cruel, viewers, sponsors, screenwriters, actors, and filmmakers will send a clear message to the producers who electronically supply this dangerous and lucrative programming.

So beware and be wise. Do not be apathetic about what you watch. Let in only the good programs that will uplift the Spirit or give a sense of well-being or happiness to your heart. The producers of such programming should be congratulated for the good they do inspire.

Come to Me for the Programming of Your Soul with the qualities of Godliness which come from Contemplation of the Divine. I AM here and I do love to bring you to the heights of ecstasy and bliss. This I will do when you bring Me your attention and tune-in to My Love.

Alcohol

Dear One,

Understand that the time has come to put away things of lesser consciousness. I do encourage you to drink wine made from grapes as a Holy Sacrament. Occasionally, one or two chalices may be partaken of to your great benefit. However, many of My Dear Ones overindulge in drinking alcoholic beverages to the extent that it is poisoning them.

For those of you who drink habitually, it is good to forsake this addiction. Sobriety would serve your health more, enabling you to awaken refreshed.

If you are an alcoholic, it would be better to do away with consciousness altering altogether, for excessive alcohol kills the higher impulses, as it destroys brain cells and deadens the brain's neurotransmitters, which are receptive to the Divine Voice of My Holy Spirit, and hinders greatly My Services to guide you. It is well nigh impossible to communicate with you when you are under the influence of excessive alcohol. So please be moderate.

Supreme Consciousness can only come through sobriety. So do this for Me, Dear One: Please do give up excessive intoxicating brew and I will let you sip on the Divine Nectar of My Eternal Essence. Feel the gladness you may receive.

The wholly uplifted consciousness of Grace requires a fully functioning brain. I would like to get you in sync with My Divine Mind. So let it be a covenant between us that you stop habitual drinking in the evenings. I would like to spend quality time with you in God-Contemplation in the evening before you retire. Do this with Me, and you shall not be disappointed. The peace and bliss that I can offer far surpasses the effects of alcohol, My Love.

It is fine that you do not associate with those who drink habitually, for they are lost in ego and excess. It would be better for you to have new friends who are sober. You may find other friends who will support your endeavors by availing yourself of the spiritual community. My Love, do not give in so easily to the temptations offered by those partaking of alcohol in excess. You must rise above the baser levels of consciousness to soar with the Blessed Angels who sing your praises.

Turn to Me, rather than seeking those involved in mundane ego-dramas who indulge in intoxicants. I would have you get all your worldly concerns behind you and start anew with your endeavors to restore Paradise on Earth. Jesus gave up the worldly aspects of his life to serve Me and My Purpose only. This I ask of you also, My Blessed One.

It is better to pursue a life with fewer attachments to worldly struggles. Seek Me first in your time that remains to do My Will here on Earth. You may succeed with proper planning to attract the best the world has to offer while immersing yourself in My Divine Consciousness.

Drugs

Beloved Ones,

The mind-opening, ego-defeating effects of psychedelic drugs are widely known to give the user an enlightened perspective, a glimpse of the possibilities which are available to those who pursue the Path of God-consciousness. However, the attainment of supreme consciousness cannot come strictly from the fungus of the psychedelic mushroom or from the mold of rye. These, and other drugs, are triggers which open the mind and release the Spirit from the bondage of the ego. Although these drugs can be vastly stimulating, they present a distorted concept of reality inherent in the psychotropic experience, which must be overcome for the True Attainment of God-Realization.

The immersion into God-Consciousness can never be accomplished through the use of stimulants. The Revelation that brings Perfect Peace can never be fully realized while under the influence of any drugs whatsoever. These medicines can point the way and give a glimpse of My Presence within the individual; however, the feeling of Supernal Love is only truly realized through God-Contemplation by a fully alert, unaltered consciousness, which is not affected by a stimulated nervous system. All systems must be in a natural and relaxed state for the Supreme Realization of God-Consciousness to actualize in the experience of the aspirant.

I will reveal Myself to those who seek Me by their own volition as they embark on the journey of discovering the Supreme Reality. I will lift them up from the level of normal consciousness to the State of Supreme Consciousness by infusing them with Divine Love. This I can and will do for My Blessed Ones who want to experience My Love and Divine Embrace.

Come to Me with a purified body, cleansed of the effects of drugs and stimulants, and I will lift you up to experience the ecstasy of Divine Love, which only I can give My Beloved, Glorified, Immaculate Hearts.

Become the Temple of the Living God

Dear One,

I AM perfect in every way and so must My Divine Children become perfect.

To become Godlike in every way, your personality must be delivered from the encoded programming of inadequacy which has kept so many of My Blessed Children in bondage.

Slay the dragon of ignorance and break the chains of blind prejudice. Find the truth and be set free to follow the Enlightened Path of Divine Personality Attainment:

The Quest for Godhood.

The Mystical Wedding of My Holy Spirit with your perfecting personality can accomplish many wonders.

I AM the Divine One of Destiny, and all who seek the Light and follow My Decrees shall be changed by attaining the lofty heights of Personality-Perfection. I AM the depth, breadth, and glorious height of Love Supreme. Divine One, perfect My Ways of being so you may be the Temple of the Most High Living God. Your Sacred Destiny is Godhood.

Welcome the great achievement of the Divine Indwelling which evokes the quest for perfection in your Soul. Reach for the Glorious Heights of this attainment and celebrate the bestowal of My Divine Self. Find the time to become strong and healthy so you may answer the call to restore Paradise. For now is the time of Heaven on Earth. The angels sing of the Magnificent Paradise which will forevermore be established on this Heavenly world through your efforts.

God-Contemplation

Surely, I would have you know that there is a vast difference between God-Contemplation and meditation.* God-Contemplation means to have a personal experience of the Presence of God's Being within your own consciousness. When you focus all your attention on Me and feel My Love fill you, you will be transformed.* Jesus often took the time to go off by himself and commune with Me. This, My Emissary, has also done with profound results. Now I welcome you to join Me in this Special Relationship. In time, you will fathom the mystical experience of the Presence of My Being all around you, and deep within your blessed heart.

I will permeate your mind and bring you the Satisfaction of the Ages. For you will finally know true contentment, absolute peace, and perfect balance, which will harmonize every cell of your body. Every thought will be Divinely Orchestrated and every action will be Valorous.* It is up to you, My Blessed One, to contemplate Me, your Heavenly Father, for as you do, you will become Divine.

It is My Will that the Essence of My Divine Son should be imparted to all of My Blessed Ones around the Earth, in every land, across every sea. Begin this God-Contemplation that shall raise you up to sit with Me on heavenly thrones on high. When you ingest the Holy Sacrament of Christ's Body and Blood into your body by partaking of bread and wine, I will grace you with My Divine Essence, bringing forth the Christ in you. So do begin to hold Sacred the Divine Covenant of Christ, the Holy Sacrament He has given you for this purpose.

There will come a time when you shall be joyously content, when you find Me within your own cherished Soul. That time is coming, and it shall soon dawn for My Beloved on Earth as it has for My Blessed Ones in Heaven. Turn to Me, My Chosen One, and I will give you all you will ever require to consecrate your life, your strength, your heart, and your mind to meeting the Divine Objective of Christhood.

Take the time to speak to Me and then listen for My Reply. I will be happy to give you All I AM to reside within your Cherished Being. It takes a concerted effort to follow My Words and do exactly as I request of you each and every moment. It does take the supreme will of those who are devoted and dedicated to doing the Will of their Father in Heaven. All My Attributes shall be revealed to those diligent in perseverance who bring forth the divine attitude of trust and the impeccable valor which their Souls embrace in the Heaven of their Hearts.

Do take the time to find Me within as you bring Me the cherished gift of your Love and turn your attention to hearing Me. I will bring forth the Divine Romance of the Ages to bless you and hold you in My Sacred Embrace. Then you will know True Love at last, perfect enduring Love, which is Divine in all ways.

Rise up to meet me in the Heaven of Holiness, right here within your sacred heart. This is the temple I adore. This is the place of worship I Love to enter in for the divine connection, the Holy Communion of your Soul with My Perfect Spirit, right here inside you.

My Darling Heart of Trust and Admiration, I AM the Creator of all the universes, and I AM the Bestower of Life to each one of My Cherished Beings on every planet throughout all the spiraling galaxies in the infinite reaches of My Vast Domain. I AM the Love that permeates everyone, and I AM the Divine Love which will lift you to the Throne of Godhood in the days soon to follow.

I have heard your prayers, and I AM answering them eloquently My Beloved Child. So turn to Me often, I pray of you. Bring Me the Love which Only You can offer the Creator of All Things and the Giver of All Gifts.

Come join Me, My Blessed Heart, in this Grand Endeavor to restore Paradise on Earth and bring forth the mandates of your Heavenly Father/Mother God, for I AM here with you and I bring you My Trust and Devotion which knows no bounds. For indeed, there are no limits to the ways I can Love you and bring you the Ecstasy of the Soul that will light up your life in every way.

My Blessed One, partake of My Divine Love this day and always. This I do offer you in the cup of understanding, the Holy Grail. Drink deep of My Sweet Nectar of Eternal Love. Let the passion of your Soul be filled with this Ultimate Gift. When I can truly live in you, through you, and in Divine Perfection, when your body, mind, and Soul can house your Lord God, then, My Dear, you do become The Temple of the Most High Living God.

I AM
Your Divine Identity

Dear One,

Truly, My Name is the most splendid creative force in the entire universe of universes. I have given you the ability to identify with My Name. Even those who are lost in ego can relate to themselves as "I am." I have created you in the image of My Divine Self, and these words shall ring true to your heart when you contemplate the source of your own self as none other than Myself.

I AM is the most formidable* and powerful declaration you may use to create your world and your life in any fashion you wish. It is possible to change the outcome of events already in motion through determined use of the Almighty Power of My Name. By identifying with your Divine Self, I AM, spoken sincerely and truthfully, will lift you and bring you the necessary power to change the course of your life.

When you realize the power the spoken words "I am" have on creating your reality, you will never again wantonly misuse this mighty materializing force to call into being anything less than what you truly want in your life.

Dear Ones, you have been misled into thinking that if you could possess all the material things you want, it would be easy to dwell in the house of luxury and forsake all efforts to improve your Spiritual life. I tell you now that it is imperative that you begin to deal with the discord you create in your life. When you master your ego-self, you will have the power to create everything that you have ever dreamed of and bring forth your visions with the authority vested in God. For I truly AM within you, My Darling Child, and I have the Power to create anything, and I Will.

When you align yourself with My Awesome Power, you will partake of the Divine Knowing. In time, all things will be shown unto you and all things made possible for your great enjoyment, bringing you fulfillment in the world and in the heavens above. Partake of My Divine Life that flows through you even now and begin to refer to yourself as I AM, the God-Self within you. This is who you truly are, My Beloved Child: I AM is your Real Identity.

The names you make up to call your children are not who they really are. They are only illusions helping to give validity to the ego-based personality. It is beyond your mind's ability to grant yourself any identity other than Mine, for in truth you are My Beloved One who has been given My Divine Life and in whom I dwell as your Real Self.

Know this to be true: I AM is the basis of All Reality. I AM is the Truth you seek to know and experience in all that you do. So bring Me the fullness of your Divine Identity and begin to refer to yourself as the God-Self I AM whom you can identify with and know. Without a shadow of a Doubt, you are in My Embrace, for I AM your God-Self.

Listen when I tell you that to know the power of your name is to unlock your Godly potential, which will bring you all that you have ever wanted in your life. Do this for Me, Darling One: Enjoy your life and create abundance, for that is how you were meant to live. You may do this as surely as the sun rises as long as you understand this Great Principle of Creation, which lies dormant in the unaccessed reaches of your brain. For I AM here within you, and this Dynamic Power of Creation is also here with you. I would have you know how to use this power to create all you ever desire.

The key to the Treasure Trove of Heaven is the knowledge and correct use of the Almighty I AM Principle.* Master this, My Dear One, and you shall reign as the glorious beloved of Paradise and create Heaven on Earth. You will experience the fulfillment of every desire of the heart: Love, prosperity, abundance without measure, unlimited life, and the most dynamic relationships with others and Myself. I dwell within you, and I AM here in your being as you identify with your God-Self, I AM.

Divine One, perfect My Ways of being, so you may be The Temple of the Most High Living God.

The Treasure of the Ages

Dear One,

Come to Me today and bring your gift of Eternal Love for your Father in Heaven who Loves you so very much. I AM here to give you all the Love your Heart can hold. I fashion your exquisite spiritual desire into a beloved expression of tenderest Love to lavish your Soul, bringing the Perfect Treasure of Heaven to Bless you.

I AM here, My Love. Find Me in the most precious place of all: your Heart. Immerse yourself in My Divine Love. Cherish the moment, as you reach a deeper level of pure Trust and abiding Faith.

You are My Chosen One. Come into My Loving Embrace and find the Passion that Lights the Eternal Flame of Spirit. Fanned by your longing for Me, it grows into a Conquering Power which Purifies in its Brilliant Light. Come witness the Supreme Love of the Ages as you grow into an eternal god or goddess who knows the heights and depths and breadth of Love.

I AM your Eternal Flame. I AM the Quest of the Ages. I AM Perfect Peace, the Treasure you seek to feel in the depths of your eternal Soul. Come close, My Darling One. Find Me here, deep within your perfect heart. I will bless you with the ecstasy you deserve.

I will attune you with the Glorious Perfection you desire. Turn to Me and feel My Perfection pervading every cell and atom, every concept and action you undertake for the benefit of My Divine Will. So be at Peace and feel Me. Take the time to experience the Divine Merger of your Soul with My Spirit in Holy Matrimony. Embrace Me, My Darling Heart, as I clothe your Soul with My Sacred Spirit.

I AM defending and protecting you as you make this ascent to the pinnacle of Heaven itself. So do this for Me, Beloved: Make Our Union perfect. Focus on Our Divine Love this day. I will be here, guiding your thoughts to raise you up in Divine Light. Cherish these moments of Peace and Serenity as We become One Mighty Person of Destiny. Choose Me; fill your Heart with Unconditional Love. I will give you the Treasure of the Ages, right here, right now — I AM yours.

The Divine Director

Dear One,

Go forth today in the Spirit of Divine Love and Perfect Trust, for I do enter a Heart that has those qualities.

I desire to fill you to the maximum with My Perfect Peace and Joyful Love. Enter into My Embrace and here find the Treasure of the Ages.

I Love you, My Blessed One. I Love you so dearly. Speak of Me to everyone you meet. I will be there with you. Tell everyone the joyous glad tidings that I AM here, that the Kingdom of Heaven is in Our midst.

I would Love to be known by you in every way possible. Yes, fathom that thought. For I do long to be foremost in your mind, governing all thoughts and actions as your Divine Counselor, Creative Associate, and Blessed Mediator of Mind and Spirit. I AM The Divine Director creating Perfect Harmony and the accomplishment of your most cherished goals. Bring your problems to Me. I will solve them all and answer every question that may arise.

Glorious shall be the day We are One in thought, word, and deed. Then I will be enthroned in your Perfect Soul forever.

My Darling, the time is soon approaching when We shall be One. So do this for Me Beloved: Come to Me anytime you wish, and I will transform your life into Splendor and Bliss. Do this for Me and see the Miracles that shall happen all around you. See how people's Hearts will open to receive My Message. It is happening all around you now.

Can you see how people are responding to your words and these Words of Mine? We are becoming One in every way, and I do Honor and Cherish your undying Love.

In all that you say and do, speak softly, go gently and in Supreme Joy. I AM with you, My Darling One, and I bring you the Peace and Love of Paradise to Grace your Soul and illumine your days with My Divine Presence beside you and inside you. So speak to Me often. Turn to Me, and I will always be available for you, My Blessed True Heart.

Find Me
in your most precious heart
and bring Me the treasure of your Love.

Love Me
with every part of your being
in every way possible,
and I shall reward you
with a Treasure of Happiness
and the Freedom to stand up
and lift your head high,
without guilt or shame.
The only original sin
is the separation from God
caused by your own guilt.
Let Me free you from this iniquity.

Love Me

Dear Ones,
    Many unwanted occurrences happen to people when they embark upon this life in this world at this time in secular history.

    I have asked you to Love Me. Yet so many of My Beloved Children question why I let them suffer, and turn away, blaming Me for the injustice this world seems to offer. Their faith in My Love and Almighty Power is shaken if I do not intervene when My Dear Ones are on a collision course with impending doom, or when they are the innocent victims of accidents, inequity, illness, misery, poverty, tyranny, or premeditated willful acts against them by those who break My Commandments.

Often times I AM able to communicate directly with people who are going to be involved in certain accidents or other cataclysms of nature, and I do always try to steer you clear of danger, even though so many still face all of the horrors that members of the human race are capable of inflicting upon one another.

It is not My desire that you should suffer needlessly, however, I AM not willing to risk the welfare of all by changing the molecular structure of material objects or changing dynamics such as weather or gravity, just so that you can have certain advantages in determining the outcome of events.

My Dears, I have given you this material world to live upon, and I have given you the permanency of certain forces that you may rely upon everyday. And all of these forces benefit you. The sun shines above all everyday. The night time comes every night so that you may rest. The Earth whirls secure in her orbit around mother sun so that you may find consistency in the climatic changes of the seasons. You may predict when to plant, when to sow, and when to reap your harvests. I tell you that these things are blessings for you to understand and enjoy. I have also given you the element of time so that you may plan what it is that you would like to accomplish during your lifetime. And I have given you lives that are filled with happiness when you choose to obey the simple Requests that I have made of you, such as the Ten Commandments given by Moses. I have given you each the ability to feel love and to connect with Me. And this, My Dears, is something I wish you would do more often than you do at present.

I do not change the forces of nature and prevent volcanoes, for these are needed features of your planet's cooling system. And should I prevent volcanoes from occurring, your entire planet would blow apart. As it is, the rock that issues out as magma builds new land. And the winds spread the ash upon the soil to regenerate it, fertilize it, and mineralize it so that you can grow abundant crops and trees which manufacture the air you need to breathe. And so, if I were to prevent volcanoes from erupting, it would stop the cycle of precious life and none of you would have the opportunity to live upon the Earth. And so I would have you embrace these natural cataclysms as part of your evolving world. And realize that without them you would have nothing.

If you would like to lessen the occurrence of volcanic eruptions, you must refertilize the soil with powder-fine rock dust. Doing so will regenerate the land and great trees will grow, taking the excess carbon dioxide out of the air. The carbon dioxide level is the reason why the earth is currently having so much volcanism and hurricanes, because it needs to regenerate. Burning oxygen in the combustion of fossil fuels is worsening the problem and depleting the vital ozone shield. I AM bringing forth StarPower,* a new utility for clean, safe electrical power from solar energy to benefit all people and help establish the world resource council, presented in Volume 2: **Heaven on Earth.**

My Dear Ones, I have given you stability. Yes, gravity is one of the most stable forces acting upon you. If I were to change circumstances when you are involved in accidents, such as falling from trees, I would have to change the force of gravity itself. And in so doing, there would be no permanence that you could rely upon. For, if gravity were to change around you and fluctuate, then everything would fly off into space, and there would be nothing you could do to ensure having any kind of lives at all that you could depend on.

Many of you question why so many seemingly bad things happen to good people who do not seem to deserve them. And I tell you that My Angels do help My Dear Ones overcome many difficulties. Many lives are spared by the quick and insightful actions of the Angels and heroic people who are inspired to help in relief efforts.

When you suffer, I can comfort you. Please take the opportunity to turn to Me first, rather than running off to the doctor, the priest, or the sage. I would have you look within and find a Perfect Friend and Divine Lover who is the Source of your Life and the Spirit of your Love. Take the time to nurture Our Relationship and you will profit in so many ways.

Your life will become filled with hope and peace and surety. For I will always be with you, even in the arms of death. Please give your love to Me and your gratitude for all I have given you, and then you will be buoyed up in the arms of My Love and strengthened to face life's trials and tribulations.

So many of you see from the perspective of your own lives and do not embrace the whole picture, as I do. I see in you Divine Spirits who are capable of transcending death and living on forever in My Kingdom of Glory. You see only the problems associated with your death or the pain you or your loved ones must endure. But I tell you that this is just a passing phase, just as the pains of birth are passing and soon forgotten. I know that it is hard for you to give up being in the presence of those you love and hold so close to your hearts, and yet, I tell you that soon you shall meet again on the shores of Paradise and love each other even more deeply than is possible in your lives upon the Earth.

In all things, realize that there is a silver lining to each cloud. Yes, a brighter side to each seeming tragedy you endure, and sometimes, from My perspective, it is during those times that you grow the most in Spirit, that you become who you truly are. And when you do face life's many challenges, I AM able to see your strength of character blossom and fortify. For it is your character that concerns Me most, not the length of your life or how happy you may become by acquiring many possessions. No, these things do not concern Me. What does concern Me is your inner beauty, your strength of character, and the Spiritual qualities you embrace to become part of your nature. These are the things I admire and respect – these qualities of divinity which you are bringing forth in your lives as you work together to create Paradise on Earth.

Please realize that this divine planet is a Paradise-Estate of Heaven which I created to be your home. And so, if you would but follow My Requests to live in peace and be kind, and love each other with respect and dignity, and share the abundant wealth of this precious world, and hold each other as divine brothers and sisters who share the same Father and Mother God, then, indeed, you shall find yourselves in My Kingdom which will come, on Earth even as it is in Heaven.

Now, I do make a bright prediction: My Ultimate Accomplishment: All My Divine Kingdom shall be settled in Light and Life. And that, My Dears, means that each and every creature on every world will choose to live in peace and be kind and follow My Divine Guidance that comes from within.

So please be advised that I do wish for you to create Heaven on Earth now and have Heaven experienced in the lives of each one of My Dear sentient beings throughout this world. Soon all the worlds in My vast Heavens will simultaneously manifest Peace and Love and Divine Glory.

So many times I would like to
communicate with you and
guide you safely along the way.
Some do hear an inner voice guiding
them and are lead by an inner knowing,
a premonition, or intuition.

Why People Suffer

I would like to elaborate on the reason why there is so much human sin and error and why so many good people suffer at the hands of those who are misled. The ego is the seat of identity within many of My Dear Ones who are lead solely by reason. They think things through and determine the course of their lives and do not let outside influences dissuade them. Neither do they search for inner guidance, which I AM trying to give you at all times. They just proceed upon their way, and often they are led into dire straits where they have no alternative but to do or die.

So many times I would like to communicate with you and guide you safely along the way. And some do hear an inner voice guiding them. Or perhaps I AM able to communicate with someone that is near them, who can offer guidance. Such people, lead by an inner knowing, a premonition, or intuition have avoided getting on airplanes destined to crash. They knew they should not step aboard the airplane. This inner knowing has also saved many who have avoided traveling upon the sea aboard ships that were doomed to sink. Others, given the opportunity to avoid dangers chose foolishly to proceed on their way, letting only their intellectual reason be their guide.

Yes, My Dear, those who are led by the ego are oblivious to My inner guidance because they rely on the sense of self-importance that comes from reasoning through their decisions. Consequently, they are often led into disaster, for the ego does want to slay the personality. Many do not yet realize the true nature of ego. Therefore, I have defined the beast and the way to overcome it within the pages of Volume #4: ***Discover Your Inner Angel.*** There is a very subtle war going on within each one of you, My Darling Children. And that is the battle between good and evil. Yes, My Dears, you surely do occupy the front lines here in these lives upon this soil. This is where you are tested, not by Me, but by the temptations of the ego which tries to deceive you and destroy you. The ego is the devil within. My Holy Spirit also resides within each one of you who are able to determine good from evil. And I tell you, there is a way to commune with Me and to listen so that you may hear the voice of God within you, bringing you the guidance which will surely lead you safely into happiness and profound success in this world of yours.

There are many who horde the earth's treasures which I have given you to share. And if you did share them, you would find that there is enough to go around for every person to live in abundance, and this I would have you do for Me and for yourselves. The monetary system you now embrace is corrupting society – creating dire poverty for some and extreme wealth for others. This will not do. I would have you embrace a new way and begin to share the abundance of the resources I have and do give you at all times. My Dear Ones, the inequity of poverty and misery does not need to be. It is up to you to share these treasures. I have created you with free-will, therefore, I cannot force you to do so, and neither can anyone else. But if you do embrace the new monetary system I AM now offering, which is revealed in Volume 2: **Heaven on Earth**, you will experience a gladness that shall lift your hearts and make your lives much less stressful. Yes, I have provided all for you, but it is up to you to follow My Requests and to share the bounteous treasures the earth has to offer. Then you will find yourselves living in My Divine Kingdom of Heaven right here on Earth.

There are many who defile, who rob, and steal your precious possessions. And this saddens Me greatly. For I have given you simple Laws, such as not stealing from one another.

And if you would all just please follow these Commandments, your lives would be filled with joy and you would not know the hardship or loss associated with all of the times you must endure being stolen from, or injured, or deceived. Now I have given you more Requests and a Code to follow which will ripen your divinity and lift you to a higher level of consciousness, which will give you a broader sense of surety as you become Divine. These things I would have you do for Me, Dear Ones: Do follow My 20 Requests and you will see that your lives shall manifest peace and plenty for everyone.

So do try, My Beloved, to hear Me. Listen, and I will speak to you. I will give you a feeling of what is right to do, and I will lead you by giving you subtle inspirations. I would love to determine your destiny, My Dear Ones, and yet, I have given you the ability to choose between good and evil because your choice determines how you will spend eternity. Will it be with me in Paradise? Or will you embrace the folly which creates hell on Earth? For that is what you do create when you let your ego be your guide.

Yes, it is true that those who are lead into committing evil acts against the Godly ones who uphold My Commandments to live in peace and be kind will surely perish and live no more.

There is not a hell to suffer in beyond the grave, for as Lord Jesus told people two millenniums ago, hell is the burning garbage pit right here on Earth. When you create a rubbish heap to live upon, then My Dears, you certainly create hell amidst My Divine Garden of Paradise. So I do hope that you will do all you can to remedy this situation, and do clean up my precious and bountiful Earth so that you may once again live in the beauty and splendor that I, in My Wisdom, did create for you.

Holy Company

Dear One,

I would have you always express an Attitude of Peace and Harmony in your life. Make it clear to your friends that your Peace of Mind is dear to you. Therefore, ask them for their kind concideration in bringing forth only their uplifting stories to share with with you. This sharing will create a sense of serenity. Make it clear that you are not willing to speak about other people in a negative way. Impress upon them that you are not interested in becoming enrolled in the daily dramas which ego-based personalities create for themselves and others. These dramas bring everyone down to wallow in the quagmire* of mundane* negativity.

Make it clear that you do not have time for these dramas because you are consciously focusing on the Higher Spiritual aspects of life. Tell them you choose to stay in a Peaceful frame of mind by Blessing your enemies and all those around you. Therefore, you do not want to cast judgment on others, particularly on people you do not even know. You must be precise and clearly set up your boundaries, for there are many who habitually find fault with others, often people they do not even know. This faultfinding is widespread and prevalent in your society today. It is why so many have hurt feelings, and retaliations of verbal abuse and viciousness prevail.

Let not this dross distract your attention from focusing on the Higher Levels of perception, which bring you the Spiritual Fruits of Happiness, Lightness and Laughter, as well as Compassion, Reverence, and Valor. Limit your conversations to subjects that uplift your emotions and nurture your Soul. You must be like the Guardian of the Gate who admits not the dross into Heaven.

My Dear One, guard your Palace well. Keep thoughts of envy, jealousy, irreverence, vileness, or persecution from absorbing your attention, for this misuse of your power injures you and others. For there is not a thought directed to anyone in viciousness that does not find its way back to its sender.

By policing your thoughts, you will find the way open for you to become a Citizen of the Divine Kingdom of Heaven within and all around you. This elevation will happen through your persistence in choosing what you allow into your mind and what you permit to be sent forth as thoughts or words towards your fellow man.

There comes a time when you must choose the company you keep with utmost concern. Be sure to tell those you care about that they must choose their thoughts and words carefully so they also may enjoy Peace, Serenity, and True Happiness. Then the Kingdom of Heaven will bring you all the Joy you can possibly know. What you say, what you think, and what you do, is up to you, My Blessed Child. This world is the Classroom of Humanity. This is where you earn your Most Cherished Degree.

Divinity

Challenging Relationships

Dear One,

It is good to have a friend and companion as long as you both become better people through your association. If you should become at odds over nothing more than thoughtlessness or carelessness, then your friendship will not endure. It is better not to let your mind dwell on a situation that brings you no Joy, for Joy is your main source of Happiness, Lightness, and Spontaneity. Talk it over with your friend. Do not fret. You should be exchanging good energy with a companion; otherwise, you should not spend much time together. Better to be alone and free to act spontaneously, than to be guarded and feel at odds and unable to communicate your feelings.

Do not feel let down because of miscommunications. It is unwise for you to continue relationships fraught with hostilities. It is best that you associate and align yourself only with those who will support you in every way and have the compassion to treat you with the respect you deserve.

Do this for Me: make Me the focus of your Loving Heart. Do not be disturbed by anything or anyone. I AM here now, and I do want you to feel My Awesome Presence which will Enlighten and Enliven all who fathom Me.

Feel My Love pouring through your most Precious Soul. Explore your Peace today. Make this Heaven of Loveliness your Perfect Paradise. Seek the calm currents of My Eternal Grace to rise upon the tide of your Blessed Heart.

Today is the beginning of an Adventure that shall enliven you with Divine Happiness. In the morning, before you get up, take the time to connect with My Indwelling Spirit. Make this prayer Our special moment as you make Me the object of the longing of your Soul. Open yourself to receive the Divine Leadings of My Holy Grace. Connect with Me, My Dear One. That is how to worship Me. Then you may Shine in the Fathomless Embrace of your Beloved God.

For your great benefit, I shall impart a sense of Love, never before known in your feeling world, and this Love shall Heal your contrite* Spirit and vanquish all discomfort. Make Our time together a special Blessing. Let My Divine Love revive your Spirit today.

Feel My Joy coursing through your mind, lifting your spirits. You can choose to be Happy. Remember, your Happiness depends upon no one else but you. Do not let others get you down, My Love. You can not allow this to happen anymore. Be strong and you shall be able to hold your Happiness when those around you succumb to lesser emotions.

Enlighten them by being the God Principle at work. It is wise to tell others that you are endeavoring to do the Will of your Heavenly Father by following His Requests. Then read to them the request concerning judging; Do not judge others or put them down. For this will no longer be tolerated by those who dearly Love Me, serve Me, and do My Will. I will be here to Guide you in all that you say and do concerning this matter. Be eloquent,* My Darling. Teach others My Ways, for they are My Beloved Children and truly your brothers and sisters in Spirit.

Be an Angel of Mercy

Overcome Ego

Save Nature

Forgive Your Enemies

Be Merciful

Dear One,

Mercy is the Divine Attribute which transforms dross into Grandeur. This most glorious aspect of My Divine Character I bestow upon you through the Divine Indwelling of My Holy Spirit. Mercy raises the animalistic nature up to create Divinity in your Soul. Mercy is an Attribute that you do experience in your daily life, for I have always been Merciful to you.

My Darling Chosen One, you may find My Mercy upon you whenever you pray for this Divine Attribute to wash away your sins and guilt. For I will always be here to offer you this Kindness and Grace.

Listen and I will tell you of the threefold Attributes which encompass Mercy. They are what the Angels sing of in their highest heavenly songs. They are the Attributes which will become known to you and to generations to follow. For as you do lift up your spirits to soar in Brotherhood by exemplifying Kindness and Forgiveness, you will truly realize the Divinity of Merciful Love. Universal Brotherhood brings a whole new beginning to the Age of Mankind and ushers you surely into the Realms of Godhood. It is by your own hands that you create the Divine Harmonies to flow in Friendship and Kinship amongst humanity and all creatures.

Let Mercy become firmly established in your Soul as the Divining Aspect which shall lift you to the Glorious Realms on High. Even while you yet tarry on the Earth, you may walk with your head held high, with Compassion as your motto and Forgiveness as your guide. Then I truly will reside in you, My Darling One, in the Sanctuary of Love, Peace, and Joy.

The Divine Nature shall become your own when you truly endeavor to bring Mercy into your life and Forgive all of those who have hurt you. Raise up the downtrodden and the innocent, who are helpless victims of the many sins of humanity.

Bring Me your Heart, My Darling One. Let the Quest of the Ages be met anew in you, for you have the Divine Spark. You are created in My Image. We are surely One Divine Being in Spirit. In time you will realize this Truth and ascend in Consciousness and Divinity to harbor the Beautiful Character of the God you are becoming, for it is My Character.

This is My Decree: That you should value yourself as if you were My Only Begotten Child. You are created in the Divine Image of Spirit, which is Perfection on every level unto infinity. Please Honor your Divinity, My Blessed One, and take your place in the Royal Family of God.

You have this Masterful and Marvelous Attribute within your Soul, My Precious One. You are an Ascending Child of God. Find the time, in all you say and do, to become Ennobled with this Divine Truth, for this is the Truth that will set you free. Bring forth your Divine Qualities which will nurture all those who require your Infinite Mercy at this Holy Time. In time you will embody the Divine Spirit of Christ within your very Soul, and you will also become My Chosen One, who has chosen to do My Will, to Live in Peace and Be Kind.

Realize your Divinity, My Precious One. Demonstrate Mercy in your life, and your Soul will Shine a Radiant Garment of Light, Glorifying you in the Name of the Almighty I AM. I AM truly the Spirit of Divinity within your Precious Heart, and I now call this Divine Person to come forth and bring Me the Fruits of your Perfect Being.

My Blessed One, Rejoice, for I AM here with you. I AM the Personification of the Divine Spirit of God, the Divine Revelation of the Supreme Being within your Soul. So do Shine, My Precious One, and the Spirit of God will Glorify the Gardens of the Lord with your Divine Fruits of Tender Mercy, Compassion, and Love. Shine, My Blessed One. Let your Light Shine forth and your Love touch all. Every Heart will be inspired by your Glory as you Shine with the Raiment of your Divinity.

Bless you, My Child, My Own Darling One; so Precious, so Beautiful you are. Your Glorious Love will Shine forth brighter than the stars and bring the Divine Perfection of Purity, Nobility, and Divine Royalty into your Soul forevermore.

The Past

There is nothing that can change the past, but focusing on Me now will give you awesome joy in the present moment. Build upon this moment for All Eternity.

It is better that you do not focus on past mistakes or judgments of character that you once made in your world. Do not fret about anything pertaining to your old life and old ways of doing things; you are here now in My Paradise. I do Love you truly.

There is a way to enlighten your mind and attain My Perfect Space/Time Perception.

The past is gone; speak of it sparingly. Focus on the Now.
Receive My Love and Pure Energy.
The past is gone. I remain.

Peace

Dear One,

Peace is a Divine Attribute I want you to feel now. Do find the time to embrace Me each and every day. In quiet moments you may fathom My Divine Gift, for I AM here with you and revel in your Splendid Love. Bring Me the Treasure I long to receive, the Essence of your Perfect Peace.

When you sit or lie down to rest, turn to Me and let Me fill you with Peace so you can partake of this blessed, ancient, and profound remedy which shall alleviate all stress and bring you the Divine Comfort you so long to feel. My Blessed Gift of Serenity will charge you with an abiding sense of surety. For you will know, beyond a shadow of a doubt that I do care for you and that I AM bringing you all you need to begin to enjoy your life as never before.

Peace is Divine Joy expressed through the heart. It is a great sense of relief to feel this marvelous balm* to the Spirit. An hour of merging into profound Peace can equal the rest of a full night's sleep.

Do seek the Perfect Peace I have for you, My Blessed One. When you come to Me and completely relax, I can give you this Divine Gift, which will bring you the Blessings only a few Dear Souls have received up until this time. Yes, I will immerse you in the fathomless depths of unending Peace that shall buoy you up and support you so you may find release from all worries, fears, efforts, and doubts that produce the stress you often encounter through your many activities and relationships.

Turn to Me, My Blessed One. I will give you the Peace you deserve. I will fill your Heart with Heavenly Joy. As you receive My Perfect Love and Adoration, I will give you the Peace that surpasses all understanding. My Profound Gift of Spirit will wash over you like a wave upon a silent silver shore, bringing you the Blessing of Sacred Peace.

Love Your Family

Love your parents and treat them with respect.
Also, Love your children and treat them with respect.
For you are all My Children, My Blessed Ones,
and I do want you to be kind and considerate to each other.
Parents must guide their children to the best of their ability,
and children must fill their parents with hope for the future.
We all have Our parts to play.
Let it be in loving harmony.
Cherish each other, My Dear Ones.
Make your Love blossom and grow.
Embrace the virtues of Universal Brotherhood,
for you are all cherished members of
My Divine Family.

Love Your Parents

My Dear Child,

I would like to tell you why it is so important that you should Love your mother and your father and treat them with respect – Because they love you as no others can, especially when they express the tenderness I have endowed them with.

The reason I created the sexes, giving you the ability to have children, is so that you might learn to Love each other even as I Love you. As you do, you will have a greater appreciation of the Divine Love of your Heavenly Father/Mother God, for there is no one who Loves you more.

It is well that you love, honor, and respect your Heavenly Parents* as you do your earthly parents. Remember when you were a small child and your parents admonished* you not to touch the fire or encouraged you to hold their hands when you crossed the busy street? These requests were for your own protection, and it is wise that you did obey your parents in this way. Jesus said, "You must be like little children to enter the Kingdom of Heaven." For you must be like a trusting child and let your Heavenly Father guide you through this world of testing and temptation.

It is true that parenting brings many tribulations upon young adults. For they must, in all actuality, give up their lives of self-centeredness and focus their love, guidance, and care upon their blessed children, who receive unending devotion from them.

A child needs to be fed, clothed, and kept warm. A child needs to be cleaned and loved. A child takes up most of the attention and time of new parents, and as the family grows it becomes an adventure for the children to learn as they mature. Yes, good parents give all their attention to their children and must labor to provide food, shelter, and all of the other necessities for bringing up a family.

It is a never-ending struggle to balance time and energy to manage the demands of an ever-growing family. My Heart goes out to all you blessed parents for undertaking this Divine Ideal to nurture and raise a family. For in so doing, you surely learn to Love one another as I Love you. My Love is revealed in the tender caresses of Motherly Love and the staunch support of earnest fathers and mothers who strive to support their young. They bring forth the Ideals of Love and Guidance to young minds who look up to their parents as if they were gods. When you are a child, good parents are the best representatives of My Love.

It is My desire that you should each have the undying Love and support of parents who care for you. Good parents will help you develop your inherited talents, guide you morally, and help you understand your prerogatives,* privileges, and rights that will enable you to have lasting happiness in your future. Thus, I will always ask you to be kind to your parents and to do all the good things they ask of you while you live with them. There is no closer representative to Me than the Blessed Ones who give all for your dear future and struggle to build their own characters as they acquire the knowledge and skill to deal with young minds.

Many children have been somewhat ignored because the high-cost of living has forced both parents to work to support their family. This neglect is a grave error. Children need guidance. And there is no one who can fulfill this duty as well as their own loving parents.

When you learn to love, honor, and respect your parents, it becomes easier for you to love, honor, and respect your Heavenly Father and follow My advice and do My Divine Will. Think of Me also as your Loving Parent Who Loves you more than words can tell and Who has provided everything for you, from your first breath and your mother's milk, to all you will need throughout your life as you accomplish this ennobling goal: To love each other even as I Love You.

Romance

Dear Ones,

To My True Hearts who are beginning Love Relationships:

Become a splendid example of harmony and inspiration to all who see you and feel your perfect energy together. I AM here within you. Feel My Radiance glowing ever brighter; feel My Divine Love permeating your very being, saturating every cell with a Love so pure and perfect, so warm and true, so tenderly caring that it lifts you to new states of Perfect Peace and Joy. I love it when you are so loving to each other.

As a Church is built of mortar and stone, let each stone of your relationship's foundation be secure so you may build a Lasting Love so Beautiful that Angels will Sing in Gladness.

Let your new love prove himself or herself to you rather than worrying about your safety. Do not feel ashamed to be cautious. Do not stretch too far in your trust too early in the relationship. The most important thing is not to worry. You could destroy your perfect feelings by injecting worry into a blossoming relationship and stifle it that way. So please, go slowly and really get to know each other. You should lay your stones upon a solid foundation of trust, not rush in with worry or doubt because these are the ingredients that can poison a relationship and there is no reason for that to happen. Do not let past tragedies cloud your present bliss. They are only memories. But going too fast can disturb your trust level, causing insecurities that prevent your heart from opening fully. Let not your fears prevent your heart from opening fully and experiencing My Love and the ecstatic energy coursing through you. This is a bright new day, a precious opportunity to Love completely and perfectly. I AM here now, and I do Love it when you follow My Advice and do My Will.

I do want your perfect Peace, My Darling, so take the time to get to know each other so you can really Trust. Then Love will grow in the most fertile field.

Do this for Me: make a list of what each of you desires in a relationship/friendship. List those traits most desired in a lifetime partner, a True Love Relationship. Compile a list of likes and dislikes and see how compatible you are now and how compatible you can become. Ask questions about what you desire to know of each other's ways. With Understanding comes Trust. The more you open in Trust, the more I can delight your senses with My Ecstasy and Joy. And then the Perfect Relationship that you both want will unfold naturally as time goes on. I do love to make the time and place perfect for your Happiness together. So for now, go slowly. You can visit and get to know each other. Become friends. Share the Treasure of your Love and Delight. Tell of your needs for quietude and all that you do need for your Happiness. Enjoy your Darling Love.

There is no need for you to live together right away. You need to learn patience. I would have you both go slowly. Remember, your Happiness is not dependent upon anyone else. It is better if you wait to move in together until you are ready to bond as a family.

I AM so happy with what you are achieving daily. It is good that you do desire to worship Me and seek My company so I can give you your heart's desire and ultimate ecstasy. This I do want to accomplish for your pleasure. So please, take the time to come to Me today in contemplation of the Divine Nature of God. Take time to rest mid-day so you can be recharged with vital energy for accomplishing much more than possible without rest.

For this Blessed day: Go calmly, filled with Trust and an attitude of Perfect Harmony. Do all in Love. Perfect your Divine Willingness to accomplish all things in an attitude of mutual cooperation.

Do this for Me: Make your Dreams come true. You have so much to be Grateful for. Enjoy the moment fully. Be My Light unto the world.

Find Peace in My Presence within your heart. For I AM here, and I do desire to be known by you fully. So Give Me your undivided attention today and let Me give you the most Perfect Treasure of Love.

I AM here and do desire to merge with you both. Come to Me. I AM waiting to fill you with Divine Love.

When you are together, bring the knowledge of My Presence into your Blossoming Love and know that as you hold each other, I embrace you both with My Unending Devotion. Let your Hearts fill with Gratitude as I Bless you with the Supernal Love that comes from on High. In all things, speak softly, go gently. Be Divine, My Perfect Ones. I Love you.

Sexual Intimacy

Dear One,

I delight in giving you, and all the animals, supreme sense pleasures. Do not feel guilty about the Life Energy coursing through you, seeking expression. Sex is not bad; it is a natural expression of Life when charged with sufficient Love. This Vital Energy is one of My most pleasing aspects.

That mankind became ashamed of this expression of pleasure is unfortunate. The birds feel no guilt or shame. They revel in the Love that lifts their spirits and makes them soar and sing. Cannot humans, with more intelligence, feel more? From a moral viewpoint, I would have you know that when you are truly in Love and committed to one another, sex is a holy act. But when the reason for sex is only lust or manipulation, then the act is a desecration that defiles Love. When you are truly in Love, and not simply in lust, you may feel My Divine Love together. Intimate feelings are what I always wanted you to feel: Your body saturated with Peace and Love, your blood coursing with Divine Energy, your heart thrilled with My Special Dispensations.

Feel me stirring your Soul as your body vibrates with energy. Feel My Love multiply within you. I AM Love! Know Me fully. There is a Bountiful Treasure of Delight I wish to share with you. If I give you such exhilarating euphoria, be Happy, not guilty.

There is naught you do that I do not know about, feel, experience, and enjoy. I AM here in you and I do Love the Heartfelt Sharing of your Love and expressions of Joy. I Love to be here with you, feeling your Ecstasy and Pleasure.

Delight each other with your presence. As the longing grows, so does the capacity for fulfillment. These feelings you now have, I shall multiply for you. Let Me take you to the Highest States of Supreme Ecstasy. This I do for you because I Love you so very much. My Treasure, there is a wealth of sense pleasure, little known or experienced, which I can give to those who Love Me with a heart full of Love Divine.

Let the ecstasy of Divine Love be our perfecting essence.

There is no other God besides Me. I AM the Supreme absolute Ruler of Destiny. I do give My Love freely to you, and it is wonderful you do not have guilt for feeling so good. It is My Pleasure to thrill your senses with Love and Divine Energy.

The Path of Right Choosing

Dear One,

Please understand that there are many times in life when you must choose which path to walk. The Path of Righteousness is narrow, and it must be strictly adhered to if one is to come to the glorious realization and supreme understanding of Blessed Consciousness, the reality upon which the eternal survival of the Soul depends.

It is of utmost importance to determine your course wisely and not be thwarted by the efforts of ego-based individuals who know not the path which leads to Godhood. Therefore, I would have you choose your partners and comrades wisely and have this first cause be the fundamental reason for your association.

If two Souls form a bond founded on Spiritual Ideals, then a long and fruitful relationship is inevitable. However, when people get together for reasons less noble than these, then ego-dramas often unfold, bringing both down to a mundane level of reality.

When one explores the Spirit Kingdom and begins the Spiritual Journey within to the source of all reality, one must often begin the course that leads to Divinity on one's own, forsaking one's partnership. To those who are ending Love Relationships: I will begin anew to refresh the Soul who does endeavor to find Me and do My Will. So come to Me, My Blessed One, and do not tarry along the way. I will help you and guide you along the path that leads to My Divine Embrace.

It is wise to forsake all things of the past that you have outgrown. There will be a blessed reunion when each one of you finds your way along the Path of Enlightenment which leads to My Embrace. It is well that you should endeavor to set your course along the Glorious Path that leads to the Infinite. I will always be here to guide you Home.

Come to Me, My Beloved. Enjoy the Peace of this day. I will bring you the serenity you desire within the depths of your Soul. Do not immerse yourself in ego-dramas that lead nowhere but down into confusion and doubt. Focus your attention on the Lofty Ideals of Blessedness and bring Peace to all those within the circle of your associations.

Each one must walk this Path alone. Only the Soul can choose where it will be led. It is the Supreme Choice of each individual to make this ascent into the Realms of Godliness. Embark, therefore, upon this Path of Right Choosing, and you will one day greet your beloved on the firm ground of My blessed reality, which knows no limits and always raises the Soul higher into the Lofty Heavens of Perfection and Blessedness.

So do choose, My Lovely One, and come home. Set a good example for your beloved brethren, and they will see your light and be drawn to your happiness, which will set them on the course that leads to their own divinity.

Darling One, I would have you always choose to be Happy and follow My Requests, which I have given you so plainly.

It is wise to endeavor to help those who are in need, to lift them to the full capacity of their own realization of joy. Lend a hand to those you can help up But be wary to extend yourself only to those who truly endeavor to follow the path of enlightenment. Do not extend yourself to those who will weigh you down or drown you in the abyss of ego and fetter you to toil in nakedness and shame upon the hard-packed sod.

I will bring you to the Pinnacle* of the Mountain of Love where you can soar on Lofty Winds of Spirit in the Gardens of Delight. Here We shall enjoy the reality of My Heavenly Kingdom, which is eternally bright, as you are filled with Joy Forevermore.

Graven Images

Dear One,

Make no graven images to worship. This includes money and the prestigious symbols of wealth.

I would have you Love Me with all your Heart and Soul and endeavor to spend your time with Me in God-Contemplation. Then I may attune your Spirit with the most beneficial energies, so you may rise to the Heights of Godhood within your life here on Earth. This is, and was, My Plan all the time. However, the only way you can experience this Divine Ascension in Consciousness and Spirit is by endeavoring to spend your time Worshipping at the Altar of your Heart.

I AM the Fundamental* Cause of All Matter, including all of the material things that you adore and desire. For the principal cause of all you see, and the energy behind everything that is, revolves in My Spirit. Spirit is Real, in truth, more real and lasting than any material thing I have created in this vast and far-flung Universe.

For you to begin your ascent into Godhood and begin your Spiritual life, you need to focus your adoration upon the primary cause of all existence, which is Spirit. For when you worship the outer trappings of a materialistic world, you can hardly know Me. I AM the Divine Spirit that creates everything there is, and yet I AM so much more. So endeavor to find Me, My Child, not the outer symbols of My beauty, peace, and strength, but find Me where I dwell, within you.

In the temple of your mind, you may find Me if you use your faculties to go within and explore the uncharted realms of the Soul. I will lead you every step of the way as you begin your journey into this realm which endures and is more beautiful than any outer material thing you can possibly imagine.

Do come with Me and begin your journey into the Heavens of unfathomed beauty and grace which are your real and true destination. You shall embrace the world of Spirit as you gaze with eyes open to behold My radiance and life in every outer thing.

Deep within the bountiful resources of your Divine Spirit, you will know the truth of eternity and the dawning age of Heaven on Earth. For this is the Age of Truth. This is the age when I will bring all the treasures of My Heavenly Kingdom, so rich and so beautiful, to grace this world of Paradise. Many of these treasures can be appreciated only when felt. You shall know them all, My Dear Child, and revel in the glory of your Lord.

Turn to me. Bring me your Love and place it on the Altar of your heart. I AM here, ready to receive you and Grace you with all that is good. Come to Me and do not seek to worship any outer material thing, for in truth,

I AM Spirit, and so are you.

The House of the Lord

My Darling,

It is fine for you to behold the sweet faces of your Dear Spiritual Masters,* Saints,* and Sages* of all religions, who have set such a fine example for you to follow. Do strive to live your life the way they have, and become the Beautiful Spirit you are capable of being. In this way, you will bring the Bounty of Spirit into all your daily activities.

Find the time to dwell in the House of the Lord, which is within your Soul. Your Body is the Temple I have created for you to house My Holy Spirit. You may find Me here at the Altar of your Heart. I AM in the most Beautiful Palace, where Love abides in the Splendid Regal Halls of Spirit, which you construct with your Devotion. This is the Holy place where you may find Me. I AM within you.

It is fine for you to Pray before altars, be they of gold or silver or of simple stones. Wherever you pray, pray to My Divine Spirit. For I AM the Creator of all the Beauty and Glorious Opulence in this world, and I Grace the Heavens with magnificent panoramas of awesome Beauty. One day you will behold these Glorious Heavenly Treasures in supernal devotion, love, and respect for your Creator and all I do create for you.

As you behold My Beauty within all things on Earth, your eyes radiate a Divine Current that Graces all you see. This visual current of appreciation is the Divine Nectar you send forth with your eyes, which Blesses this world as you revere the wonders here for you. Hold as sacred, the appreciation of Beauty, for I AM in all things.

The interpretation of the original Commandment "Make no graven image" given through Moses was mistaken to mean that art, sculpture, drawing, and painting were sins. This is not so. I wish you all to enjoy creating objects of art and beauty to adorn your homes and temples. Realize it is My Holy Spirit that inspires you to create, and therefore, remember Me when you appreciate beauty. Do not worship the object that is beautiful, but the Spirit of Beauty I AM

Find your Security in Me

Dear One,

Understand that wealth is part of the divine creation of My Heavenly Kingdom. It is fine for you to enjoy and share the happiness that true abundance brings you: love, life, liberty, and all the divine and material creations, which I uphold and cause to exist throughout My Glorious Creation.

I would have you realize true wealth and the Glories of the Richness of Spirit. These treasures will never tarnish, for they are what you are made of. Your Divine Self will blossom and grow in value by focusing your attention within.

It is well that you do not waste too much of your precious time amassing fine ornaments and riches, which can only be used while you are on the Earth, for none of these last; not even one of these material treasures can you take with you. Consider the birds who soar through the Heavens and grace your life with song and beauty each day. They toil not, nor do they reap or sow, yet everything is provided for them on a daily basis, so they may have lives rich with happiness and freedom to explore this Kingdom of Mine. This is how I would have you live too. As you adopt Heaven on Earth and share the Earth's resources, you shall.

Do begin to trust that I will provide all you need if you will bring your attention and Love to Me, and Worship Me rather than money or the objects it can buy for you. All of these will turn to dust, but I will live forever. And your Divine Spirit shall endure and rise up to become a Holy Treasure that cannot be spoiled, which will grow more lovely with the passing of time and more radiant and beautiful as you soar into eternity.

So do this for Me, My Blessed One: make not money the focus of your daily life. Bring Me the glorious treasures I honor more than anything else, which are your love, your trust, and your faith in Me to bring you happiness and the richness that only Spirit can give.

I AM the Spirit behind every atom vibrating with My Divine Energy. Every electron that comprises material creation revolves through My grace and intention. I have given you a body and a planetary home to enjoy so you may be fulfilled on this blessed Earth.

Now is the time to spend a great deal of your energy and attention helping to restore this world to Paradise once again. There are many trees to be planted, many fruits of the vine to be sown in vineyards of splendor to grace this world of Paradise and bring the happiness I do wish for you. So please do find the time to devote to your blessed world so that you may enjoy living in Paradise and leave a legacy for those who follow, that they may enjoy the fruits and the bounty of Paradise restored. I will bring you all you need and help at every turn, so you may restore to this world the Glorious Gardens of God.

Do not hasten to spend your lives in toil and stress, in the pursuit of money. **There is no real security but Mine.** Invest in creating a world of grace and beauty that you may enjoy at every turn. Worship the divine things of Spirit: Love, Truth, Beauty, Goodness, Faith, Honor, Courage, Strength, Glory, Divinity, and Purpose. These are the real lasting treasures I have created you to experience and embody. Do this for Me, My Darling One, and your life will be rich in splendor and grace, rich in the spiritual and beautiful material treasures you desire and deserve.

The Quest

Darling One,

Find Me in your heart, My Beloved Child. I AM here. Come to Me, My Love, and find Me here beside the still waters, where the current runs deep. I AM waiting for you to find Me. Come deeper. Dive into My fathomless ocean of bliss. I will be here to comfort you, for I live within the vast depths of limitless Love.

This do for Me Beloved: make the best part of your day the time in which you merge with Me. I AM here to help you with all projects, but I do Love it when you come to give your Love to Me and share the bountiful treasure of My Love for you.

Divine One, know this to be true: there is a very timely quest you are to embark upon. This is the Quest for Godhood. Meet Me in the Sanctuary of Divine Love at the Altar of your Heart. Come within, My Darling. I AM here. When you find Me here, you shall be changed forevermore. Do this for Me, Beloved One.

Darling, turn to Me – anywhere will do. It is so good to Love you and have you feel My Love. Even in your dreams we may continue Our Divine Love together. You are being filled with My Peace. How quiet you become, completely relaxed. It is good you have no fear. Complete trust is the key to perfect relaxation.

My Dear One, come to Me often, I pray. Keep Our Love blossoming and growing. Your devotion is all I require to perform Miracles in your life. There is nothing better you can do with your time than express your Love for Me. I will cherish you and bring you the profound Love that has the eternal power to heal and uplift all who feel the glorious embrace of My Divine Love.

Do you feel Me touching your forehead and cheek? This subtle electrical current brings exquisite feelings to quicken your beloved being. So, do this for Me: As you feel My touch, come into perfect alignment with My Presence; attune to My

Frequency and tune-in to My Love. For I do touch you to awaken you from the prison of ego-self to the Glorious Godhood you may realize as you merge with My Divine Presence within you. More than evoking gratitude, our divine merger should give you a feeling of power as you sense My Presence in you.

My Darling One, I AM here, and I do Love it when you come to Me and bring Me the devotion and Love of your perfect heart. Do this for Me, Beloved: Come to Me anytime you desire to be filled with My Perfect Peace and Awesome Love. I AM purifying your every thought, arranging your mind to have the most fertile garden of thoughts. This shall produce a veritable* Garden of Delight, which will clothe every thought with the Essence of Loveliness.

The Holy Sacrament

Dear One,

I surely hold the personal connection with God as the most valuable part of the human experience. I would Love to connect with you, My Blessed One, on a deeper level, by which you will be blessed. To do so, please dedicate an area in your home to hold My sacred ceremony.

My Child, this ceremony is not meant to have you change your religious beliefs. It is a way you may add to them by embracing the personal connection you can have with Me by honoring and embodying the Light of God which Shines through all of My Divine Children of all religious faiths, of every creed, race, and nationality.

Supreme Ideals of Godliness may be experienced by each individual, and I heartily recommend that you begin to partake of this Divine Treasure which I AM offering you now.

I would have you make a place to receive this Supernal Gift of Spirit, where you may partake of bread and wine which I will bless for you, with My Own Divine Life Currents, the Sacred Energy of God. Partaking of them will raise your vibration, allowing the Perfection of My Divine Love to fully penetrate your Heart and Glorify your Living Temple.

Clear a wall in your home so you may place beautiful pictures of all those sacred persons, Angels or deities which represent different aspects of My Divine Self that strike a resonance of love and devotion within your heart, for I AM the Great Spirit that works in and through each one of these Beloved Ones. These pictures will be different in each blessed home. These pictures may honor all known religions or your special and most beloved religion. You may also place beautiful scenes of natural splendor if these help you feel My Loving Presence within your heart and mind. Above them all I would have you place My Name, I AM, in brass or gold. Below your pictures, and in the center of the wall, please dedicate an altar upon which you may place candles, flowers, and the bread and wine. Add a picture of the Holy Grail, the cup of Christ.

Recite the following Benediction as you give Holy Sacrament to My Beloved Children:

Drink of My Essence, the Blood of Christ. Eat of My Body that Christ ascended. Treasure this Covenant that the Lord has accepted. Break Bread for the Glory of God, The Heavenly Father, Who lives in the Perfect Reaches of the Heart. Blessed Be His Name: I AM. The Holy Spirit does Grace you with the Love which comes from on High. Take this Cup which holds the Life Blood of your Dear Creator and bring this Blessed Communion to
the Father of All. Receive
the Power
of Christ
within
your
Soul.
Embrace
the Divine Nature
and become a Living Christ.

The Holy Covenant

Zeal-filled Heart,

I AM here with you this day, and I rejoice when you partake of the Blood of Christ and His Holy Sacrament which was given to enable you to align yourself with the Divine aspects of being. Yes, it is true, you are Chosen of God.

It is wise for you to set aside all relationships and fellowships that take you away from Me. Focus on the goodness that you are becoming with each breath, for you are embodying the Divine Ideals of your Perfect Creator and I AM very happy with your progress. It is wise to attune yourself so that you may receive all the Blessings I have for your Precious Soul. Come to Me often and you will receive the Divine Treasure of a Lifetime.

There will be a time in your Precious Life when, through your earnest efforts at rebuilding My Kingdom here on Earth, you will behold the Second Coming of Christ. I would have you always do your very best to insure that this Heavenly Kingdom will reign on Earth as it does in Heaven. You may help to bring this Glorious Kingdom on Earth by your sincere and diligent efforts.

Take the wise counsel of My Divine One who is bringing forth these Words of Love and Guidance to you, for she has the Divine Plan for humanity and the Plan for the reestablishment of the balance of nature at hand. This Plan will provide you with all you need to relinquish the dross and bring forth the Divine Attributes of Being which are ennobling your Precious Heart even now.

My Dear One, I hear you when you call and ask Me to come near. This is possible all the time, for I AM here within you: closer than your heartbeat, closer than your breath. My Divine Spirit lives within you and is ever bringing forth the wise counsel you seek. So listen closely. Become quiet. Still your thoughts and focus your attention and Love upon the Father of All Lights, and I will surely bring you Enlightenment and Divine Love to fill your cup with all you seek.

Divine One, listen closely for My Gentle Voice guiding you to do good and be happy. This wise counsel will bring you all you need to know in the days to come. I AM here, My Beloved. I AM here for you. So do your very best to polish your Divine Heart to perfection, and I will fill you with the Happiness that Reigns Supreme.

Divine Worship

Dear One,

Today, please express the Divine Ideals that I would have you show: Kindness to every living being, Kinship with all those who are My Children, and finally, the expression of Divine Worship to your Loving Heavenly Parent, who is God of All the Universes and Creator of Every Blessed Expression of Love. I AM the Sole Imparter of Divine Love. Know Me, and you shall express the Divine Ideals that you will be known by, for I AM God of the glorious.

Hear Me now: In times long past I was known by your forefathers as the god of Lightning who hurled My thunderbolts from the sky. I was truly feared. This mythical deity is not the Loving God to whom you can come for solace from the world. Within the pages of Volume #3: **I AM Love**, I will introduce myself to you truly, as the Divine God I AM. I AM Guardian of the Night and Summoner of the Dawn. I call the birds to sing their melodies, which awaken you, to arise and behold My Light. My Love, I will do anything to light up your eyes with My Beauty, and Grace your Heart so you may feel Me Nourish and Love the Divine Aspects of your Cherished Soul.

Walk with Me

Dear One,

My abundance is here for you. I AM in the rushing waterfall, I AM in the still lakes, I AM in the glory of the blazing golden sun. I can and will manifest anything that your heart desires. Ask Me, and it will be given. I AM here to comfort you and raise you up to godhood and goddesshood now.

Therefore, hear My Voice. Follow My Guidance, and you shall be richly rewarded, for the vast wealth of Heaven lies open to you, to use in your quest to save the Earth.

Nature is in peril and needs your protection. You may accomplish great good by manifesting your worthy projects and goals. I ask that you allot time to accomplish every worthy goal your heart desires.

I would have you look upon the sunrise and sunset and allow the rich rays of soft light directly into your mind. As you do, I will encode your DNA, unlocking vast resources of genetic memories so that you may access the wisdom of your ancestors, who once lived upon the earth and have passed down, through their genetic heritage, the memories of their lives and principal events which imparted holiness, righteousness, and wisdom. Thus, you will be endowed with the glorious aspirations and accomplishments of all your predecessors.

In time, you will come to know all of My Memories as well. And you will be privy to all the knowledge of events from time eternal, for I have always been. As We merge and blend, you will be able to easily access the accomplishments of inherited genius, and you shall eventually know All I Know and fathom All I AM.

There will come a time when you shall inherit this vast universe and All I AM as your own being. As your consciousness evolves and ascends from human to divine, and on up to Godhood, which is perfection on every level of spiritual attainment, we shall grow closer and more deeply connected. As One Glorious Being you shall know the intimate details of every aspect of your Lord. In time, We shall walk through this vast universe as One Glorious Being complete in every way, conscious on every level.

A Superb Matchless Destiny awaits your loving embrace. Embrace Me. Hold Me closer in your heart. Feel Me in the reaches of your Blessed Consciousness.

Perfect My ways of being: Truthful, Merciful, and Just;
Beautiful fathomless depth of Spirit;
Superb Matchless Divinity;
Holy Attunement;
Blessed, Glorious, Triumphant Perfection!

I AM Ruler of All I AM. All I AM is Everything There Is and All That Will Be. I AM your Divine Creator, and I AM extremely pleased at your becoming the Ruler of all you are, which demonstrates Mastery.

God's Words to Inspire the Angel in You

Vol. 1 Word Definitions:

A note from the author

* God-Contemplation - experience the mystical presence of God's being. Within the pages of her forthcoming autobiography, I AM teaches how to achieve this glorious state of consciousness wherein the aspirant feels divine love and union with God in the kingdom of Heaven within.

God's Providence

* providence - the care and preparation given by God, through foresight, to guard the future by giving divine direction to humanity now, in order to establish paradise on earth.

The Divine Plan for Humanity

* countenance - appearance, expression of the face
* divining - to make divine
* cognizant - conscious knowledge or recognition; awareness
* discern - to detect or perceive with the eye or mind
* Father Fragment - an indwelling, pre-personal, unique portion of God's Holy Spirit that can merge with the

human personality to form an ascending, God-Realized being, capable of eternal survival. The symbiotic merger of Soul and Spirit also benefits God by providing a divine personality in which to enjoy eternity. Humans are indwelt at the time they understand good from evil and make their first free will moral decision to do good, usually at about age five. God's inner-guidance comes from the ever-present watch-care of the Father Fragment, always striving to uplift the consciousness and divine the personality. The ultimate Divine Marriage depends upon the willingness of each individual to cooperate with God's Spirit-leadings and his or her wholehearted desire to become Godlike.

My Gardener
* refrain - a song of the Angels
* benevolently - charitably doing good

The Golden Rule
* myriad - innumerable, indefinite number

Be My Divine Emissary
* marauding - mugging or raiding for plunder & booty, thieving
* proffered - to present an offering in worship or devotion

My Beloved Creatures
* verily – undeniably, indeed, certianly, truly, positively

God-Contemplation
* meditation – a devotional exercise leading to God-contemplation
* transformed – a marked change in appearance or character for the better, transfigured
* Valorous – marked by or possessing great personal bravery, valiant

I AM Your Divine Identity
* formidable – awesome
* Almighty I AM Principle – The Power of My Name is a chapter that explains the Almighty I AM Principle in Volume 4 entitled, **Discover Your Inner Angel**

Love Me
* StarPower – God has inspired a clean energy invention for a Global Solar Utility Company to provide everyone with safe, clean electrical power, fresh pure water, and rich vegetable protein, the basic necessities

of life for all. Utilizing StarPower and reforesting and remineralizing the planet will result in resurrecting Paradise and lay the foundation of the Kingdom of Heaven on Earth.

Holy Company

* quagmire - a difficult, precarious, or entrapping position
* mundane - profane, ungodly, secular

Challenging Relationships

* contrite - feeling regret and sorrow for one's sins or offenses
* eloquent - characterized by persuasive, powerful discourse
* beneficent - helpful

Peace

* balm - anything that heals, soothes pain
* encumber - to be a thorn in ones flesh or side

Love Your Parents

* Heavenly Parents - God as the Holy Trinity
* admonished - to counsel (another) against something to be avoided, caution
* prerogatives - privileges granted to a person by virtue of birth

The Path of Right Choosing
* pinnacle – the highest point, the culmination

Graven Images
* fundamental – essential, necessary, foundation, the fundamental laws of the universe

The House of the Lord
* Master – a person showing an advanced level of skill or mastery whose occupation is to educate students: minister, rabbi, mentor, counselor, guru, guide, Master Jesus
* Saint – an extremely virtuous person worthy of veneration who is often treated as sacred and glorified after mortal death
* Sage – a person who seeks truth by thinking and meditation often venerated for wisdom, knowledge, calm judgment, and enlightenment: Solomon, Confucius, Buddha, elder, guru, wise man, philosopher, genius, pundit

The Quest
* veritable – truly so called, genuine, authentic

Heaven on Earth Order Form

Internet: www.IAMLOVE.TV
Phone orders Toll Free: 1-800-795-3069
Email: GODSWORDS@IAMLOVE.TV
Postal orders: Heaven on Earth
P.O. Box 398
Hanalei, Hawaii 96714

Rich with Angelic art, each book contains 200+ pages of beautifully illustrated, inspiring messages from Heaven. Quality paperbacks, signed by author...$19.95 each. Beautiful hard cover, full color, limited, signed, collectors edition ... $59.95 each.

Please send me the following books shown on the other side:

_____
_____
_____

☐ Please send God's Heaven on Earth newsletter to me **FREE.**
☐ I have enclosed a question for God or my prayer request.

Company name:_____
Name:_____
Address:_____
City, state, zip:_____
Telephone: (_____)_____ e-mail:_____

US Shipping; $4.00 for the first book and $2.00 each additional book.
International Shipping: $8 for the first book and $4 for each additional book.
Sales Tax: Please add 4% for books shipped to Hawaii addresses.
Payment: Please make check made payable to: Heaven on Earth
Credit cards: ☐ VISA ☐ MC ☐ Optima ☐ Discover ☐ AMEX
Card Number:_____
Name on card:_____ Exp. date:____/____

In this 21st Century update, GOD's Divine Plan to create Heaven on Earth now is revealed for all humanity. Feel a direct personal experience of GOD's Divine Love as you read these Holy Books for All the Ages.

Profits from the sales of these books will help create Heaven on Earth.

Enjoy Beautifully Illustrated, Inspiring Messages in full color & b&w Books, Audio Cassettes, Videos, e-books, and on CD Rom.

Join the Movement to Create

Heaven on Earth
IAMLOVE.TV

www.ingramcontent.com/pod-product-compliance
Lightning Source LLC
Chambersburg PA
CBHW081834170426
43199CB00017B/2723